Recipes

TO

Kill

FOR

A DESERT SLEUTHS
COOKBOOK

Recipes TO Kill FOR

A Desert Sleuths Cookbook

DS Publishing
Scottsdale, Arizona

DS Publishing
Recipes to Kill For

Book design by Maegan Beaumont
Cover design by MW Designs
Cover photo by Depositphotos

Print format ISBN: 978-0982877470

Dear Reader ~

Fasten your aprons, it's going to be a hot recipe you'll never forget. In these pages you'll explore delectable and devilishly tasty recipes that are, without a doubt, to kill for. Keep in mind that's to kill *for* not die *of.*

The dinners and desserts in the following pages contain combinations of ingredients both familiar and exotic and include something for every gastronomic taste. Forty-one of our members offered one or more recipes; it's a mystery where they all came from, but our investigation leads us to believe they originated in our members' imaginations or maybe from their grand-mothers' memories, or maybe from the old dude who lived next door. But, we have to thank Susan Budavari, Merle McCann, Maegan Beaumont, and Yvonne M. Corrigan-Carr for their inspiration to create the book and doing all the detail-intensive, coordinating-maddening, and editing work it took to transform that inspiration into reality. And that's not all. They had to fight the desire to cook and taste all the recipes they handled.

Desert Sleuths created this book because we wanted to show off not only our storytelling skills, but also our culinary talents. Oh, don't get us wrong. Our members spend their days hunched over their computers spinning tales of mystery, murder, and mayhem. But, by night they're hunched over their cauldrons brewing concoctions that when served up, promise that something wickedly good this way comes.

Happy reading and happy dining ~
Katherine Atwell Herbert
2019 President, Sisters in Crime Desert Sleuths Chapter

Dedication

To
All the writers who are great cooks,
All the cooks who aspire to be great writers,
All the readers who savor delicious food and a great
story!

Acknowledgments

The Sisters in Crime Desert Sleuths Chapter wishes to recognize the many individuals whose contributions made possible our first ever Desert Sleuths cookbook.

Our sincere thanks go to:

The Desert Sleuths members and 2019 *WriteNow!* Conference speakers who graciously contributed their treasured recipes and writing tips;

Susan Budavari and Merle McCann, the editors and co-chairs of this project, for their diligence in preparing the submitted recipes and writing tips for inclusion in this volume;

Past President, Maegan Beaumont, for her clever cover and interior design, and for formatting the manuscript for publication;

Katherine Atwell Herbert, President of Sisters in Crime Desert Sleuths Chapter, for valuable insight and guidance;

Beta readers, Lauren Buckingham, Margaret C. Morse and R K Olson, who read the manuscript for errors and omissions; and

Yvonne M. Corrigan-Carr, who provided logistical assistance on all aspects of the project.

Editors' Note

The recipes and writing tips included in this volume were generously offered by members of the Sisters in Crime Desert Sleuths Chapter and by our esteemed speakers at the 2019 *WriteNow!* Conference.

Many of the recipes are old family treasures, and personalized remarks follow them. Others are fresh takes on familiar dishes. The recipe titles have been designed to reflect the mystery and writing-related theme of the book.

The recipes are divided into Main Dishes and Desserts and are grouped by subcategories (*See Table of Contents and Index*). The editors have made every effort to present the recipes in an easy to follow format. In certain cases, the name of a particular brand of ingredient is listed which the submitter has found works especially well in the recipe.

A minimum number of abbreviations have been used; all are listed in the Table of Weights & Measures on page 223, which may prove of value to cooks everywhere. Also, please consult the USDA "Basics for Handling Food Safely": https://tinyurl.com/jcx3lw4

The writing tips are ones the submitters have found especially helpful during their writing careers. They are listed in a section at the back of this volume and are arranged in alphabetical order by the last name of the submitter.

If some of these recipes catch your eye, give them a try. Chances are you'll find yourself adding them to your list of favorites. And we hope you'll find gems among the writing tips that will aid you in your writer's journey.

TABLE OF CONTENTS

MAIN DISHES

MEATS & SEAFOOD

DESSERTS

CRISPS, CRUMBLES & NUT BREADS

PIES & PASTRIES

PUDDINGS & CHILLED DESSERTS

Main Dishes

Notes

Meat
&
Seafood

Notes

CHICKEN CATCH-A THIEF-ATORE

Serves 6

Ingredients:

3 lbs boneless, skinless chicken thighs
½ cup flour
salt and pepper to taste
3 Tbsp olive oil
1 large red onion sliced thin or diced
1 - 8 oz can tomato sauce
1 tsp crushed red pepper flakes
½ lb sliced Portobello mushrooms (I add regular sliced mushrooms to make up the ½ lb)
1 green bell pepper finely chopped
½ cup sliced black olives
¼ cup chopped celery
1 tsp kosher salt
1 - 14½ oz can diced Italian tomatoes
½ cup Barbera wine (I use Sangiovese. It is Italian, made by Bolla).

1) Heat the olive oil in a heavy skillet.
2) Combine the flour, salt and pepper in a gallon sized zip-lock bag. Add the chicken thighs and toss to thoroughly coat.

3) In the skillet, brown the chicken on all sides.
4) Place the sliced onions on the bottom of a large crockpot or slow cooker. Add the browned chicken thighs.
5) Combine all the rest of the ingredients. Stir together and pour over the chicken.
6) Cook on low heat 7 to 9 hours (or on high 3 to 4 hours).

Prepare your favorite pasta the way you like it. (I like it also with mashed potatoes.) I serve the cacciatore over it with a lovely bottle of Barbera or Sangiovese.
Use the crockpot to slow-cook this savory meal and win compliments!

Recipe submitted by RP Dahlke

CHICKEN & MUSHROOMS CRÊPES CONSPIRACY

Preheat oven to 350°

Ingredients:

2 Tbsp vegetable oil + 2 Tbsp oil for baking pan
8 Tbsp butter
½ cup of flour
1¼ cups of milk
1¼ cups of chicken broth
¼ cup chopped shallots
¾ cup sliced white button mushrooms
2 cups diced cooked chicken
¼ cup dry sherry
salt and pepper
¼ cup Parmesan cheese
8 packaged crêpes (can sometimes be found in the produce section of your supermarket) or homemade crêpes (recipe follows). Filo dough cut to resemble a crêpe can be substituted.

1) Sauté shallots in oil until translucent. Stir in chicken and mushrooms, cook 3-4 minutes.
2) In a separate pan, stir flour into melted butter, season with salt and pepper. Over low heat, stir

until the flour becomes golden. Whisk in milk, sherry, and broth. Bring to a boil.
3) Set aside ½ cup of sauce. Mix remaining sauce into chicken mixture.
4) Put one-eighth of chicken mixture into the center of each crêpe. Fold over, put folded side down in an oiled baking dish. Spread reserved sauce over the top and sprinkle with Parmesan cheese.
5) Bake at 350° for 15 minutes.

Basic Crêpes Recipe:
1 Tbsp vegetable oil
1 cup flour
2 eggs
½ cup milk
½ cup water
¼ tsp salt
2 Tbsp melted butter
1) In a large mixing bowl, whisk together the flour and the eggs. Gradually add in milk and water, stirring to combine. Add the salt and butter; beat until smooth.
2) Heat a lightly oiled griddle or frying pan over medium high heat. Pour or scoop the batter onto the griddle, using approximately ¼ cup for each crêpe. Tilt the pan with a circular motion so that the batter coats the surface evenly.
3) Cook the crêpe for about 2 minutes, until the bottom is light brown. Loosen with a spatula, turn, and cook the other side.

As served in my novel, Revenge for Old Times' Sake, a Tracy Eaton mystery.

Recipe submitted by Kris Neri

CHICKEN POT PIE TO KEEP THE PEACE

Serves 4

Preheat oven to 425°

Ingredients:

5 Tbsp butter
¾ cup small chopped white onion
5 Tbsp flour
½ tsp salt
1 tsp pepper
1 tsp ground rosemary
1 ¾ cups low sodium chicken broth
½ cup cream (half and half or whole milk will do, but
    the peace guarantee is off)
2 ½ cups shredded chicken
2 cups mixed frozen vegetables, thawed
1 cup frozen corn, thawed
1 sheet puff pastry, divided into four squares

1) Place puff pastry squares onto an ungreased cookie sheet and bake per package instructions, usually 15-20 minutes.
2) In a 2-quart saucepan or pot, melt butter over medium heat.
3) Add chopped onions and sauté until tender, usually 4-5 minutes.

4) Add flour, rosemary, salt and pepper, and whisk briskly until flour is well blended, usually 2-3 minutes.
5) Slowly stir in chicken broth and cream, whisking briskly as you go to avoid divorce-inducing clumps. Raise heat to medium-high and allow mixture to come to a bubble while whisking.
6) Once the mixture is smooth, add shredded chicken, mixed vegetables, and corn.
7) Stir mixture until well combined and let it come to a bubble again. Remove from heat.
8) Spoon mixture into individual ramekins. Place baked puff pastry square on top of ramekin and serve.

The magic of this chicken pot pie is that it not only tastes divine, but it also looks and smells incredible. The build-up of adding the various ingredients, the smell of the flour as it turns nutty and the rosemary's floral notes waft through the steam of the bubbling mixture, and the final placement of a golden brown, crusty puff pastry pillow tilted lovingly on top of it all parallels brilliantly to the magic of writing.

Recipe submitted by Deborah Lewis

CHISELER'S CHICKEN AND DUMPLINGS

Serves 2 to 4

Ingredients:

2 chicken breasts
2 chicken thighs
½ white onion, chopped
4 stalks celery, chopped
3 carrots, peeled and sliced or ¾ cup frozen peas
1 – 2 Tbsp olive oil
¼ tsp marjoram
2 Tbsp chicken broth powder or bouillon cubes
3 Tbsp butter
3 Tbsp flour
Salt and pepper to taste

1) In a large pot, cook chicken in enough salted water to cover the pieces. Remove chicken, cool and remove skin and bones.
2) Pour broth into separate container and wash original cooking pot.
3) Sauté onion and celery in olive oil in clean pot. Return broth to pot.
4) Add vegetables and chicken cut in large bite-sized chunks.
5) Simmer together with marjoram, chicken broth powder and butter.

7

6) Taste and adjust seasonings with pepper and salt if needed.
7) Shake 3 Tbsp flour in a jar with ½ cup cold water and slowly stir into broth. Cook, stirring until liquid thickens slightly.

Dumplings:
2 cups Bisquick
⅔ cup milk

1) Mix Bisquick and milk in medium bowl. Drop by tablespoonfuls into lightly boiling broth.
2) Cook uncovered at a simmer for 10 minutes. Cover with lid and steam for an additional 10 minutes.

Serve with green salad.

A family favorite by unanimous vote. Although it's a common dish, I discovered the secret to fluffy dumplings completely by accident. When I tried to "fancy up" the cooking pot so I could serve to company, the dumplings would be soggy. The secret is to use a large pot with plenty of "head room" between the surface of the food and the lid of the pot. Makes a great comfort food on a cold winter night.

Recipe submitted by Toni Niesen

DETECTIVE O'CONNOR'S PINEAPPLE BOURBON CHICKEN WITH ORANGE CILANTRO RICE

Serves 4 to 6

Preheat oven to 350°

Ingredients for Pineapple Bourbon Chicken:

4 skinless, boneless chicken breasts
6 oz butter
1 tsp Spanish paprika
1 tsp lemon pepper
½ cup brown sugar
1 - 20 oz can pineapple tidbits in pineapple juice
1 - 20 oz can crushed pineapple in pineapple juice
½ tsp. each – cardamom, nutmeg and cinnamon
½ tsp. salt
½ cup bourbon (or, to taste)

Spray 13" x 9" glass baking pan with cooking spray and set aside.

1) Trim any excess fat or bone from chicken breasts. Rinse and pat dry with paper towel.
2) Melt butter in heavy skillet over medium-high heat, until it starts to bubble. Stir in paprika and lemon pepper.

3) Sear each side of chicken breasts in hot butter, just until brown.
4) Remove chicken from skillet and place in glass baking pan.
5) Drain pineapple juice from the can of pineapple tidbits. Set pineapple juice aside.
6) Melt brown sugar in butter. Add pineapple juice, stirring until mixture is smooth and translucent.
7) Reduce heat to medium. Stir in cardamom, cinnamon, nutmeg, salt and bourbon.
8) Stir in crushed pineapple and pineapple tidbits until thoroughly mixed.
9) Pour pineapple/bourbon mixture over chicken breasts. Bake at 350° for approximately 30 minutes until internal chicken temp reaches 165°.

Serve over Orange Cilantro Rice.

Ingredients for Orange Cilantro Rice:
1 - 14.5 oz. can Swanson chicken broth
⅔ cup orange juice (no pulp)
3 tsp very finely chopped fresh cilantro (stems work best for this)
2½ cups Minute Rice

Five to seven minutes before serving:
1) In a large saucepan, bring chicken broth and orange juice to a boil.
2) Add cilantro and rice and stir so both are well mixed. Cover and remove from heat.
3) Let stand 5 minutes or until liquid is absorbed, then fluff with a fork and serve.

Detective Mike O'Connor is the lead detective in my short story "Shadow Prey" and the upcoming HiLT Squad series.

Recipe submitted by Yvonne M. Corrigan-Carr

MURDER ON THE MENU: PROSCIUTTO CHICKEN

Serves 6 to 8

Preheat oven to 350°

Ingredients:

5 cups penne pasta – uncooked
3 cups heavy cream (or half and half to lighten the calories)
12 oz cream cheese, softened and cubed (1½ packages)
9 oz shredded Swiss cheese, divided
½ tsp onion powder
½ tsp garlic powder or garlic salt
¼ tsp pepper
salt to taste
3 cups cooked chicken breast (substitute dark meat, or mix half and half)
4 - 5 slices prosciutto (makes ¾ cup when cooked and crumbled)
6 slices bacon (¾ cup when cooked and crumbled) *
3 Tbsp dry bread crumbs

* This can be used in addition to or in place of the prosciutto but I often use both.

1) Cook pasta according to package directions for al dente. Drain. Meanwhile, cook the prosciutto until crisp, let cool and then crumble.
2) Cook the bacon until crisp, let cool and then crumble.
3) In large saucepan, heat cream and cream cheese over medium heat. Stir occasionally until melted and smooth. Stir in 1 cup Swiss cheese, onion powder, garlic, pepper and salt (to taste), until blended.
4) In a large bowl, combine chicken, prosciutto, bacon (if included), cheese sauce and pasta. Transfer to greased 9" x 13" baking dish. Top with remaining 1 oz Swiss cheese and bread crumbs.
5) Bake uncovered at 350° for 18-22 minutes.

Special Notes:

I grill the chicken breasts myself adding Italian seasonings but you can use pre-cooked chicken. Prosciutto is a salty Italian ham, so be careful with any added salt in the recipe.

If frozen, thaw in the refrigerator, then bake until heated through. You may need to add extra sauce if it should appear dry as pasta tends to absorb liquids. If so, you can make a quick Alfredo sauce to pour over the top.

Quick Alfredo Sauce:
½ cup butter
8 oz package cream cheese
2 cups milk
6 oz grated parmesan cheese

1) Melt butter in saucepan. Add cream cheese and stir until melted and smooth.
2) Add parmesan cheese and stir until melted and smooth.

This recipe is a huge hit with my family and friends. Although labor intensive it's well worth the time. If preparing for two, put into two 8" x 8" freezable pans. It's good as a leftover and from frozen.

Recipe submitted by L. A. Keller

Notes

_____
_____
_____
_____
_____
_____
_____
_____
_____
_____
_____
_____
_____
_____
_____
_____
_____
_____
_____
_____
_____
_____
_____
_____
_____
_____
_____
_____

VAMPIRE PROOF 40 CLOVES OF GARLIC CHICKEN

Serves 8

Ingredients:

3 whole heads of garlic, about 40 cloves
8 bone-in, skin-on chicken thighs
Kosher salt
freshly ground black pepper
1 Tbsp butter
2 Tbsp olive oil
3 Tbsp Cognac or brandy, divided
1½ cups dry white wine
2 Tbsp all-purpose flour
2 Tbsp heavy cream
4 Tbsp chopped green onion or scallions for garnish

1) Separate the garlic cloves and drop into boiling water for 60 seconds. Drain garlic and peel. Set aside.
2) Dry chicken with paper towels. Season with salt and pepper on both sides.
3) Heat butter and oil in large pot or Dutch oven over medium-high heat.
4) In batches, sauté chicken in the butter and oil, skin side down first, until nicely browned, 3-5

minutes on each side. Turn with tongs or a spatula, don't pierce skin. If butter and oil is burning, turn heat down to medium. When a batch is done, transfer to a plate and continue to sauté all the chicken. Remove the last chicken to the plate.

5) Add all of the garlic to pot. Lower heat and sauté for 5 -10 minutes, turning often, until evenly browned. Add 2 Tbsp Cognac (or brandy) and the wine, return to a boil, and scrape the brown bits from the bottom of the pan.

6) Return chicken to pot with juices. Cover and simmer over lowest heat for 30 minutes, until chicken done. Move chicken to a platter and cover with foil to keep warm.

7) In a small bowl, whisk together ½ cup of the juices from the pot and the flour and then whisk it back into the remaining juices in the pot. Increase heat, add remaining Tbsp Cognac (or brandy) and the cream, and boil for 3 minutes. Salt and pepper to taste. Pour the sauce and the garlic over the chicken. Garnish with chopped green onions. Serve hot.

This recipe is to die for. Your guests will literally swoon over this fragrant, flavorful dish and may fight to the death over who gets the last tasty bit.

Recipe submitted by Erynn Crowley

ALAFAIR'S MEATLOAF

Serves 6 to 8

Preheat oven to 350° (juicier meatloaf) or 425° (drier meatloaf)

Ingredients:

1½ lbs ground beef (or ground beef and pork
  combination)
2 cups corn flakes
1 cup home canned tomatoes with juice
1 egg
¼ cup minced onion
salt and pepper to taste

1) Combine all ingredients in a large bowl. Squish together with your hands until thoroughly mixed. (This is a disgusting process, unless the cook needs to deal with unresolved aggression or can delegate the task to an eight-year-old assistant, who will probably enjoy it very much.)
2) Pat into an ungreased loaf pan. Bake in a fast oven at 425°for one hour for a drier meatloaf, or in a medium oven (350°) for 1½ hours for a juicier one.

Variation: Substitute 1 cup milk for tomatoes and 1 cup dry bread cubes for corn flakes.

Meatloaf recipe is from The Old Buzzard Had It Coming.

Recipe submitted by Donis Casey

COP ON THE CORNER'S FAVORITE

Serves 6 to 8

Preheat oven to 350°

Ingredients:

1½ lbs ground beef
5 slices Dave's Killer Grain Bread, diced in ½" cubes
3 eggs
Mrs. Dash Garlic and Herb (as desired)
1 pkg of Lipton's dry onion soup and dip mix
1 tsp minced garlic
salt and pepper (optional)
sliced mushrooms (optional)
½ chopped sweet onion (optional)
⅔ cup milk or enough to bind together

Topping:
¼ cup brown sugar
¼ cup milk for drizzle

1) Line loaf pan with foil for easy handling and easy cleanup.
2) In a large bowl, mix together all but topping ingredients.
3) Spoon into lined loaf pan.

4) Using large spoon, create a wide gulley down the center of the loaf.
5) Liberally sprinkle brown sugar over the surface and into the gulley.
6) Drizzle just enough milk over sugar to melt it.
7) Bake one hour at 350°.
8) When eating, taste before adding catsup or other sauce. (I prefer it sauce-free as the brown sugar adds a very nice flavor.)

A spoonful of sugar makes . . .

This recipe evolved to encourage my little children to eat meatloaf. I let them taste brown sugar and showed them how I was using it on the unbaked meatloaf. Both were eager to eat it after that. Best part, we all loved it—even the cop on the corner!

Recipe submitted by Merle McCann

KILLER ITALIAN MEATLOAF

Serves 4

Preheat oven to 350°

Ingredients:

1 beaten egg
1 lb ground beef
1 - 8oz can pizza sauce
1 cup shredded mozzarella cheese
¾ cup uncooked oats
¼ cup water
½ tsp. oregano
½ tsp. basil

1) Combine all ingredients except ¼ cup pizza sauce in large bowl, mix.
2) Place in loaf in a baking dish. Bake at 350°for one hour.
3) Top with remaining sauce.
4) Let stand for ten minutes.

Recipe submitted by Lauren Buckingham

Notes

SCOTLAND YARD'S TAM O'SHANTER

Serves 4

Ingredients:

1 lb lean ground beef or ground turkey
1 medium white onion, chopped
1 clove garlic, minced
3 cups fresh spinach, stems removed
1 cup sliced mushrooms, optional
2 eggs, beaten
juice of 1 lemon
2 tomatoes, each cut in 6 wedges
salt and pepper

1) Cook meat in non-stick skillet. Add onion, and garlic and cook until softened. Add mushrooms and sauté briefly. Season to taste.
2) Wash spinach and add to the skillet. Cook until just wilted. Tie lemon halves in cheesecloth and squeeze lemon over all (or make sure to remove seeds).
3) Stir in eggs and stir until set. Check seasoning and serve on plates surrounded by tomato wedges.

Fast, easy, low carb recipe adapted from a favorite entrée served years ago at a restaurant that no longer exists.

Recipe submitted by Toni Niesen

TEMPORARILY RESTRAINED BEEF TERIYAKI

Serves 4 to 6

Ingredients:

2 lbs round steak, cut 1" thick
1 small onion, sliced
1 tsp ginger
2 tsp sugar
½ cup soy sauce
½ cup orange juice
½ cup cooking oil
1 clove garlic, chopped
cooked rice

1) Cut steak into thin slices (1/4" thick or less) and place with onion slices in a shallow baking dish.
2) Blend ginger and sugar. Stir in soy sauce, orange juice, oil and garlic.
3) Pour marinade over the steak coating all the slices well. Cover and keep in the refrigerator overnight.
4) Drain off the marinade and reserve.
5) Weave steak strips on skewers. Put the skewers of meat on a rack in a broiling pan and place about 4 inches from the heat.

6) Broil 4 to 6 minutes, turn, brush with marinade and broil until it reaches the desired tenderness and doneness.
7) Serve on the heated rice.

This recipe is part of my feeble repertoire of family dinners I prepared when my children were still actual children. It was fast and easy—the two requirements for anything I attempted in the kitchen. My worktable in the kitchen might have had a more interesting history than slicing round steak, but my postman never rang twice.

Recipe submitted by Katherine Atwell Herbert

WATCH YOUR FLANK STEAK

Serves 4 to 6

Ingredients:

1 flank steak, about 2 lbs
¼ cup vegetable oil
¼ cup lemon juice
2 Tbsp soy sauce
2 tsp sugar
½ tsp each salt & pepper
2 cloves crushed garlic
¼ cup chopped parsley

1) Score steak deeply, place in shallow pan.
2) In food processor (or blender) combine the rest of ingredients.
3) Pour marinade over steak.
4) Refrigerate overnight, or longer.
5) Bring to room temperature, drain and reserve marinade.
6) Grill steak 5-7 minutes on each side.

To serve: Slice steak on diagonal. Boil reserved marinade and pour over sliced steak.

Recipe submitted by Roni Olson

Notes

A PATSY FOR PORK CARNITAS

Serves 4 to 6

Preheat oven to 300°

Ingredients:

3 lbs boneless pork shoulder or 4 - 5 lbs of bone-in pork
    shoulder
spice rub (see below)
¾ cup orange juice
water to cover (about 2 cups)

Spice rub:
1 tsp salt
1 tsp chili powder
1 tsp cumin
1 tsp garlic powder
½ tsp black pepper

1) Cut pork into 1 to 2-inch cubes, trimming off
   large sections of fat (a little fat and marbling is
   good).
2) Whisk the spices for the rub together in a large
   bowl. Toss pork pieces with spice rub.
3) Heat a Dutch oven or other heavy-bottomed,

oven-ready lidded pan over medium-high heat with just enough vegetable oil to cover the bottom.

4) Brown the cubed pork in the Dutch oven. When the meat is browned, deglaze the pan's bottom with the orange juice, stirring to break up the brown bits.

5) Cover the meat with water until it's nearly submerged and bring to a simmer. Once the water is simmering, cover the pan and place it in the oven at 300°.

6) Stir pan after 1 and 2 hours. The pork should be very tender towards the third hour.

7) After 3 to 3½ hours remove all the pork to a platter, leaving the liquid in the pan.

8) Place the pan back on the stovetop and bring liquid to a boil. Allow it to reduce by more than half.

9) Tear pork into smaller pieces using two forks or your fingers, discarding any gristle.

10) Turn your broiler to High and place a rack toward the top of the oven. Toss the now shredded pork with some of the reduced braising liquid and spread in a single layer on a sheet pan. Broil the pork for approximately 5 minutes per side until the outside begins to caramelize.

Serve!

It makes amazing tacos, but there is no wrong way to eat carnitas.

Recipe submitted by Sharon Lynn

HIDDEN EVIDENCE CABBAGE ROLLS

Serves 4 to 6

Ingredients:

1 small head of cabbage (2 lbs)
1 cup cooked rice
1 lb ground pork
1 – 14.5 oz can diced tomatoes in tomato juice
salt, pepper, paprika, crushed red pepper flakes
1 large onion
2 Tbsp canola oil
2 tsp diced garlic
1 - 15 oz can Bavarian sauerkraut
8 oz carton sour cream

1) Remove the core of the cabbage. Boil the cabbage in a 6 qt pot filled a quarter of the way with water, separating leaves as they soften. Remove each softened leaf from pot and set aside to cool. Cut larger leaves in half along the rib. Wash and dry the pot.
2) Dice onion and sauté in the pot in oil until onion is soft and shiny. Add garlic and sauté additional 2 to 3 minutes. Add 1 tsp paprika, mix and simmer.

3) Meanwhile, combine pork, rice, juice from the can of tomatoes, salt, pepper and crushed red pepper flakes in a bowl.
4) Place a heaping tablespoon of mixture into each cabbage leaf and roll into triangular cone shape. (You can adjust the yield of cabbage rolls by varying the amount of stuffing per cabbage leaf.)
5) Place cabbage rolls in the pot on top of the onion and garlic mixture. Sprinkle 1 tsp paprika, 2 Tbsp diced tomatoes, and some crushed red pepper flakes, if desired. Slice remaining cabbage leaves into ½" strips and place on top. Add ½ can sauerkraut and 2 cups water.
6) Cover and cook on low heat for 1 hour or until cabbage rolls are soft.

Serve a dollop of sour cream with each portion of 3 to 4 cabbage rolls.

This is a variation of stuffed cabbage, a traditional dish in Hungarian and Polish cuisines.

Recipe submitted by Susan Budavari

SAVE YOUR BACON-WOVEN PIZZA

Serves 2 to 4

Preheat oven to 400°

Ingredients:

1 package (12 slices) thick bacon
1 cup (or more) shredded mozzarella cheese
2 to 3 Tbsp chopped red onion
6 halved grape tomatoes
¼ cup Parmesan cheese
a sprinkle of granulated garlic

1) Line a baking pan (cookie sheet with sides) with parchment paper or foil.
2) To form the crust, lay out 6 pieces of bacon horizontally. Make sure they are touching each other side by side. Cut the other six pieces in half.
3) Lift every other long piece (#1, 3, 5) and fold halfway back. Pick up one short piece and pull it on each end to stretch it. Don't rip it. It should be long enough to lay over the 3 long pieces that aren't folded back. Place the short piece in the middle of the long pieces. Fold the long pieces back down. Fold up #2, 4, 6. Pull on a short piece to stretch it. Place it over the flat long pieces.

Fold the long pieces back down. You should now have a woven mat started.

4) Continue the weave until all the short pieces have been stretched and placed in the woven grid. The long pieces will stick out a little. I fold the ends over or under to complete the edge.

5) Place a wire cooling rack on top of weave to keep the bacon from curling or shrinking too badly. (Sometimes I forget to do this. It's not crucial.)

6) Bake 25-30 minutes at 400° until the bacon is browned and crisping, not burned. Pour off as much grease as you can.

7) Sprinkle the mozzarella cheese over the bacon crust. Arrange the onion and the tomato pieces evenly over the cheese. Sprinkle with garlic and Parmesan cheese. Bake another 10-15 minutes until the cheese is melted and starting to brown.

8) Use a metal pizza cutter to slice.

Use any usual pizza toppings you like. Tomato or pizza sauce can be used but I find it makes it wetter than I like.

Recipe submitted by Judy Riddlesworth

SIX-HOUR PORK a la HANDS-OFF WRITER

Preheat oven to 310°

Ingredients:

1 untrimmed boneless pork shoulder (sometimes called butt)
2 large Granny Smith apples
a decent slug of booze – sherry, tawny port, sweet white wine, hard cider, marsala . . .
a handful of sage leaves
salt and pepper
4 Tbsp butter

Set oven to 310°, or your crock pot on high, then turn to low once heated.

1) Mix the salt, pepper and butter to a paste. Add snipped up sage leaves.
2) Peel and core the apples and cut into thin wedges. Lay the apple wedges in the base of a deep, sturdy dish with a close-fitting lid (or your crock pot).
3) Pour in booze, stopping before the apple floats.
4) Place the pork, skin side up, on top of the apple. Rub the seasoned, herby paste over the meat, tucking some in around the edges.

5) Cover the dish and cook for six hours. (Four hours is fine. So is eight.) Lift the meat out.
6) Pour the rich apple sauce (that now exists, like magic) into a jug.
7) Put the meat back in the dish, cover, and set it aside to rest somewhere warm for twenty minutes. (At this stage, you could slice off the skin and blast it under a hot broiler if you like to eat it crispy.)
8) Take the fat off the top of the sauce with a separator or a spoon, as it rises. Mash any remaining bits of apple.

This is best served with some plain rice, potatoes, bread or pasta to soak up the sumptuous juices, and a side of steamed green vegetables. Leftover meat can be gently reheated in leftover sauce.

Shin of beef (with beer and onions in place of sherry and apples) or shoulder of lamb (red wine and dried apricots) are both good given the same treatment, but nothing approaches the silky unctuousness of the pork.

Recipe submitted by Catriona McPherson

HOLY MACKEREL, IT'S GRILLED

Ingredients:

1 - 1½ to 2 lbs Norwegian or other mackerel (except
  King mackerel)
1 Tbsp of olive oil
1 Tbsp Za'atar seasoning
1 sliced lemon

1) Buy the fish fresh and have it cleaned and scaled.
   Back home split the fish almost all the way so it
   opens like a book. Clean any dried blood or
   entrails out with cold water.
2) Dry the fish thoroughly. Mix the olive oil with the
   Za'atar and spread over inside and outside.
3) Let the fish to rest while you turn on the grill.
   Make sure the grill is cleaned and oiled then heat
   to high (usually takes about 10 to15 minutes on
   a gas grill).
4) Place the fish skin side down. Close the grill for 4
   minutes. Flip the fish for another two minutes
   with the cover open.

Serve with lemon slices.

Check out your Asian fish market for fresh mackerel. Frozen whole fish is another option. I serve with sautéed Japanese eggplant or broccoli and brown rice. Za'atar is a Middle Eastern seasoning found in Asian stores and can be made at home. Recipes abound on the internet.

Recipe submitted by Howard (Doc) Carron

MATT'S UNDERCOVER SHRIMP AND SCALLOPS

Serves 6 to 8

Preheat oven to 300°

Ingredients:

1 lb raw shrimp (extra-large or colossal size)
1 lb raw scallops
salt & pepper, to taste
½ tsp crushed red pepper flakes
½ tsp Italian seasoning
2 Tbsp chopped shallots
2 Tbsp butter
2 Tbsp olive oil
2 Tbsp grated garlic
¼ cup dry white wine
juice of ½ lemon
½ cup thick spicy marinara sauce (either jar or
    homemade)
2 Tbsp or more grated Parmesan cheese
1 lb box spaghetti

1) Clean shrimp and scallops and dry with a paper
   towel.

2) In a large frying pan, heat butter and olive oil. Sauté chopped shallots for 1-2 minutes.
3) Add shrimp and scallops one by one and sauté. Sprinkle grated Parmesan cheese on top while sautéing.
4) Add garlic, Italian seasoning and crushed red pepper flakes to pan. Mix and sauté 3 minutes longer.
5) Add wine and lemon juice and mix. Add marinara sauce and turn heat down to simmer.
6) Meanwhile boil spaghetti until al dente.
7) Add drained spaghetti and ¼ cup spaghetti water to frying pan and toss with seafood. Add additional cheese and garlic, mix again. Simmer for 3-5 minutes longer or as desired.

Plate and serve immediately, or keep warm in a 300° oven for up to 20-30 minutes, if desired.

Matt Merano, a central character in my Merano & Bell Novel Series, prepares this dish for a sentimental dinner with his wife, Dr. Elise Bell, in REASON TO HIDE.

Recipe submitted by Susan Budavari

SWIM WITH THE FISHES SALMON

Preheat oven to 400°

Ingredients:

1 salmon fillet large enough to serve your family
Progresso Italian-style Bread Crumbs
Mrs. Dash Garlic and herb seasoning
butter, margarine or mayonnaise (full-fat style in order
    to melt in)
juice of 1 or more fresh lemons

1) Place salmon fillet on an ungreased, foil-lined pan.
2) Slather it with butter, margarine or mayonnaise as if frosting a cheesecake until covered.
3) Sprinkle bread crumbs heavy enough to cover butter, margarine or mayonnaise well.
4) Sprinkle garlic and herb seasoning over crumbs.
5) Place in 400° oven for 12-13 minutes. If the filet is large, more time may be necessary. Test for doneness by flaking with a fork. When done, remove from oven, pierce fish liberally with a fork and squeeze lemon juice over all.

Serve with your favorite rice or pasta and green or fruit salad.

This low-salt recipe evolved between my mother and me during my many visits with her in Juneau, Alaska. She and I loved to cook together. My dad was a commercial fisherman, so when I'd arrive in town, he always had lots of fresh-caught seafood on hand.

Recipe submitted by Merle McCann

Southwestern

Notes

BLAZE'S BLAZING HOT CHIPOTLE CHICKEN

Serves 6

Ingredients:

6 medium chicken breast halves, cut in bite-sized pieces
4 Tbsp taco seasoning
3 Tbsp olive oil
¾ cup chicken broth
1 medium onion, chopped
4 medium garlic cloves, minced
8 oz cream cheese, room temperature
3 cups half and half
1 to 3 medium chipotle peppers in adobo sauce, minced
½ cup sour cream

1) Sprinkle 2 Tbsp of taco seasoning on chicken pieces and mix so seasoning is evenly spread.
2) Heat 2 Tbsp olive oil in large pan. Sauté chicken pieces until cooked, about 10 minutes.
3) Mix remaining 2 Tbsp taco seasoning in chicken broth. Pour over chicken and let it come to a boil. Simmer ten minutes. Remove chicken from pan.
4) Heat remaining 1 Tbsp olive oil in same pan. Sauté onion until wilted. Sauté garlic with onions briefly, about 1 minute. Remove pan from burner.

5) In food processor, blend cream cheese and 3 cups of half and half until well mixed. Blend in sour cream.
6) Put chicken back in pan with onions and garlic.
7) Pour sauce over and bring to a simmer. Cook, stirring often, ten minutes, to let flavors blend.

Serve on rice to soak up sauce. If desired, sprinkle with cheddar cheese.

Blaze is a character in my Petra Rakowitz series. He's Petra's familiar, a red-winged blackbird.

Recipe submitted by Margaret C. Morse

CON ARTIST CHILI RELLENO CASSEROLE

Serves 6

Preheat oven to 325°

Ingredients:

8 slices of white bread
2 small cans chopped mild chilies
½ cup Monterrey jack cheese
2 cups sharp Cheddar cheese – shredded
2 cups milk
green scallions (optional)
¼ tsp garlic powder
2 tsp salt
2 tsp oregano leaves or ground oregano
½ tsp paprika
6 eggs
1 cup each frozen corn and/or zucchini sliced thin (optional)
chili powder

1) Trim crusts off 8 slices of firm white bread. Butter one side and place buttered side down in rectangular casserole dish.
2) Sprinkle 2 cups shredded cheese over bread.

3) In blender, combine eggs, milk, salt, paprika, oregano, and garlic powder.
4) If you prefer, add optional ingredients, frozen corn and/or zucchini, to blender and mix them in.
5) Pour blended mixture over cheese.
6) Top with jack cheese, paprika or chili powder or green scallions for color.
7) Cover and chill at least 4 hours or overnight.
8) Bake uncovered at 325° for one hour or until top is brown and middle is firm.

Can be served warm or cold.

Recipe submitted by RP Dahlke

DINAMITA DELICIOSOS FRIJOLES NEGROS CON FRUTA

Serves 6 to 8

Ingredients:

1 lb of dried black beans
3 ripe bananas
mango to taste
pineapple to taste
1 Tbsp, at least, of cumin
2 white onions, sliced
2 cloves of garlic
32 oz of low-sodium chicken broth or vegetable broth.
2 Tbsp butter
2 Tbsp honey or to taste

1) Soak black beans in 8 cups of water overnight. Rinse them a few times during the evening and start with a fresh pot of water each time. Leave them on your counter.
2) The next day around noon, fill a good-sized pot or crockpot with the soaked beans. Add 3 cups of broth and 3 cups of water. Add the onions, garlic, and cumin. Add whatever else comes to mind.

3) Check beans about an hour before serving. Add more water or broth if they seem dry, and leave the lid off if too watery. Adjust the cumin.
4) Ten minutes before serving: Slice ripe bananas, fresh pineapple and mango. (Plus anything else you can think of.) Sauté them quickly in butter and honey. Turn off the heat.
5) Spoon the beans onto flour tortillas or into soup bowls.
6) Put the fruit on top and add a bit of sour cream if you want. Make it pretty.

Before exploring Central America, I had never tasted black beans. WOW! They're healthy and they are beautiful.
This freezes well. You can add cooked pork or chicken to the mix. Beef tastes awful with black beans.

Recipe submitted by Meredith Blevins

"E" IS FOR EVASIVE ENCHILADAS

Serves 6 to 8

Preheat oven to 350°

Ingredients:

2 lbs boneless chicken breasts
1 - 14.5 oz can chicken broth
1 lb fresh tomatillos, husks removed, coarsely chopped
 (~ 2 cups)
4 to 5 garlic cloves, peeled and halved
1 large yellow onion, coarsely chopped
1 - 4 oz can diced mild green chilies
salt, pepper
1 fresh habanero chili pepper with seeds (aka Scotch
 bonnet)
1 - 4 oz can diced jalapeño peppers
1 - 16-oz jar *Sprouts Organic* Green Chili Enchilada
 Sauce
6 flour or corn tortillas
16 oz shredded Colby & Monterey Jack cheese blend
sour cream

1) Spread out chicken, breast side up, in slow
 cooker. Cover with broth. Add tomatillos, garlic,
 onion, and diced green chilies. Sprinkle salt and
 pepper. Cover and cook on HIGH for 3 hours.

2) After 3 hours, lightly crush the habanero chili pepper. Add to slow cooker. Cover and cook on HIGH for one more hour. (Chicken will separate easily when pulled with a fork.)
3) Lightly grease a rectangular baking dish, 11" x 7" x 1½", with non-stick spray.
4) Move cooked chicken from slow cooker to a glass bowl. Cover with foil.
5) Reserve ¼ cup of broth from slow cooker. Discard all remaining ingredients. Place cooked chicken back into slow cooker. Turn to WARM. Shred cooked chicken inside the slow cooker. Add ¼ of the reserved broth. Cover to keep warm.
6) Lay tortillas on countertop. Evenly distribute shredded chicken among tortillas. Sprinkle diced jalapeños on top of chicken, if desired. Sprinkle half the cheese blend on top of chicken.
7) Roll tortillas, place in baking dish, seam side down. Pour entire jar of Green Chili Enchilada Sauce over stuffed tortillas. Sprinkle remaining cheese blend on top.
8) Cover casserole dish with aluminum foil. Bake for 15 minutes at 350°.
9) Remove foil and broil for 5 - 7 minutes or until cheese bubbles and begins to brown.

Serve with sour cream.

This recipe begins in a slow cooker and finishes in the oven, making for a satisfying weekend meal with family and friends. You can adjust the spiciness by reducing/omitting the habanero and/or jalapeños.

Recipe submitted by C.W. Miiller

WRITERS' WEEKNIGHT CHICKEN ENCHILADAS

Serves 4 to 6

Preheat oven to 350°

Ingredients:
4 lbs boneless skinless chicken breasts
1 medium onion, chopped
2 - 8 oz blocks of cream cheese
1 - 16 oz jar of salsa verde
1 - 2 oz can of diced green chili
1 - 2 oz can of diced jalapeños
1 - 28 oz can green enchilada sauce, divided
4 cups cheddar cheese, divided
1 bunch green onion, chopped (optional)
24 corn tortillas
vegetable oil or cooking spray

1) Layer chicken, onion, cream cheese, salsa verde, green chilies and jalapeño peppers in a crockpot and let it cook on low for 6-8 hours.
2) Once chicken mixture is cooked, shred chicken and mix in 2 cups cheese, making sure all ingredients are incorporated. Once done, set aside.
3) Layer corn tortillas on a baking sheet and spray them with cooking spray before heating them in

the oven at 350° for 5-8 minutes—until tortillas are soft and pliable.

4) Once tortillas are soft, let them cool a bit before rolling.

5) When tortillas and chicken mixture are slightly cooled, coat the bottom of a large casserole dish with ½ cup enchilada sauce.

6) Spoon chicken mixture evenly into the middle of each corn tortilla and roll before layering into the dish.

7) Once all enchiladas are rolled, top with the remaining enchilada sauce, cheese and green onion before baking at 350° until cheese is melted and golden brown.

8) Pair with refried beans and Mexican-style rice to round out the meal.

Traditionally, when making enchiladas you dip your corn tortillas in hot oil to soften them to make them more pliable for rolling. If you're looking for something a little healthier, try using the above method with the oven instead.

Recipe submitted by Maegan Beaumont

Pasta
&
Dumplings

Notes

DOC'S SCANDALOUS SPAGHETTI FRA DIAVOLO

Serves 10 to 12

Ingredients:

1 lb spaghetti
½ cup olive oil
¼ lb guanciale or smoked bacon, sliced in ¼-inch pieces
¼ lb salt pork, cubed
10 dry bay leaves (or 4 fresh leaves)
1½ cups onion blended to puree (1 large onion)
2 medium onions chopped coarsely
7 to10 cloves garlic, sliced thick
½ tsp freshly ground black pepper
3 – 28 oz cans Italian tomatoes, crushed by hand
    (San Marzano or Glen Muir)
1 cup tomato paste
½ tsp crushed red pepper
½ cup chopped fresh Italian parsley
1 cup dry red wine (Chianti or Cabernet Sauvignon)
1 Tbsp fresh oregano, minced
¼ cup fresh basil, chiffonade (finely sliced)
¾ lb hot Italian sausage
½ lb sweet Italian sausage (or 1 lb Italian sausage
    ground meat)
additional fennel seed to taste

freshly grated Pecorino Romano and Parmigiano
Reggiano cheese

1) Cook the sausage in a cast iron pan on medium
heat turning often to brown on all sides.
Alternately, sauté ground sausage meat until no
longer pink and drain.
2) In a large enameled pot (4 to 5 quarts) heat the
olive oil and render the bacon and salt pork. Do
this separately if you do not wish to use the
bacon and salt pork to finish the sauce. Remove
and drain on paper towels.
3) Add the onions and sauté over medium heat for
10 minutes then add the garlic and continue until
both the onion and garlic are light yellow to
golden brown. Add the pureed onion and stir
well. Cook until almost brown.
4) Stir in the tomato paste making sure you
incorporate the onions and garlic into the tomato
paste and cook it for about 2 minutes, constantly
stirring. Add the tomatoes and all the juices. I
crush them in the can slightly.
5) Add the wine, salt, pepper, bay leaves, oregano
and half the basil. Bring to a boil and reduce to a
simmer.
6) Cut the cooked hot Italian sausage into ¼ inch
slices then quarter, and the sweet Italian sausage
into ¼ inch slices, and add to the sauce. (Or add
the sautéed ground sausage.) Add the bacon and
salt pork at this point if you'd like. Add half the
parsley. Cook for 2 hours, uncovered, on medium
low, stirring occasionally.
7) Check for seasoning and add crushed red pepper,
fennel, and salt and pepper if needed.

8) Cook 1 more hour (on medium low) or until the sauce has been reduced about an inch. Add rest of parsley and basil just before spaghetti is finished.
9) Cook the spaghetti in 4 quarts of salted water until al dente. Drain and mix with ¼ cup of the sauce to prevent sticking.

Serve with a mixture of 1 part Pecorino Romano and 2 parts Parmigiano Reggiano cheese freshly grated.

If you pierce the sausage, do it before they get too hot or you'll get sprayed with hot oil!

Recipe submitted by Howard (Doc) Carron

Notes

FORGED GREENS AND CORNMEAL DUMPLINGS

Serves 4 to 6

Ingredients:

¼ lb fatback or salt pork (or bacon, but that's cheating)
2 lbs greens, torn
1 lb turnips, peeled and quartered
2 ½ quarts of water
1 tsp salt

1) Bring the water to a boil in a large pot. Add fatback or salt pork, greens, turnips and salt. Reduce heat and simmer, covered for two hours.
2) Remove the meat and discard. Dip out one cup of the broth (pot liquor) to make dumplings.

Dumplings:
1½ cups yellow cornmeal
1 tsp baking powder
½ tsp salt
½ cup flour
1 tsp sugar
3 Tbsp melted butter
1 cup pot liquor
1 beaten egg

1) Thoroughly combine cornmeal, flour, baking powder, sugar, and salt in a mixing bowl.
2) Stir in the melted butter and one cup of pot liquor. Stir in the beaten egg.
3) Spoon the batter by rounded tablespoons into the simmering greens. Cover and simmer 30 minutes more, or until the dumplings are cooked through.
4) To serve, ladle soup, greens, turnips, dumplings, and all into bowls and dig in.

This is a very old-fashioned dish. Yes, country women did cook their greens this long, and no, it didn't remove all the nutrients. The nutrients are in the broth! Any kind of greens can be used for this delectable dish, but turnip greens or collards are a traditional summer choice. Before cooking, wash the greens thoroughly in cool water to remove grit. Cut off any roots and damaged parts of the leaves. Rip the greens off the stalks by hand and tear into strips. Turnip greens are exceptionally nutritious, but they have a peppery bite and can be bitter. To mellow them, blanch them first for 10 minutes or so in a couple of cups of water (then discard the blanching water). From: The Drop Edge of Yonder.

Recipe submitted by Donis Casey

MAC THE RIPPER

Serves 6 to 8

Preheat oven to 350°

Ingredients:

4 Tbsp salted butter
¼ cup milk
½ cup cream cheese
2½ cups shredded cheddar cheese
1 cup shredded mozzarella cheese (plus ½ cup for sprinkling on top before baking)
16 oz elbow macaroni

1) Follow directions on the box to boil elbow macaroni until fully cooked (8-12 minutes). Strain and set aside.
2) In a large saucepan, melt the butter and milk together. Once warmed, add cream cheese, cheddar cheese, and 1 cup of mozzarella cheese. Stir constantly until melted together.
3) Add cooked macaroni to the saucepan and mix until fully incorporated into the cheese sauce.
4) Dump the cheese sauce with the macaroni into a glass or metal baking pan. Sprinkle with the remaining ½ cup of mozzarella.

5) Bake at 350° for 15 minutes, or until cheese on top is fully melted and lightly browned.
6) Remove from oven and serve.

Recipe submitted by Jess Lourey

TORTELLINI TO DIE FOR

Serves 4

Ingredients:

10 oz pkg of fresh, stuffed tortellini from refrigerator
  section of grocery store (chicken & cheese, 3-cheese,
  or prosciutto & cheese work well)
2-3 dashes of sea salt
10 oz container Alfredo sauce (from dairy section, not
  canned or jarred)
5 slices prosciutto or bacon
¾ cup chopped walnuts
10 oz bag of frozen peas

1) Chop walnuts into small pieces. Measure ¾ cup
   and set aside.
2) Place prosciutto on plate with paper towels over
   and under prosciutto. Microwave on high until
   crisp. If using bacon, fry or microwave bacon
   until very crisp and drain on paper towels.
3) Crumble prosciutto/bacon into very small pieces
   and set aside.
4) Per package directions, cook tortellini in gently
   boiling salted water just until done. Do not
   overcook. Drain tortellini in a strainer.

5) While tortellini cooks, warm the Alfredo sauce on low heat in saucepan until heated through.
6) Microwave peas to al dente stage. Drain any water off peas.
7) Place tortellini in a serving bowl. Gently stir in ingredients in order: warm Alfredo sauce, peas, walnuts, crumbled prosciutto or bacon.
8) Serve hot.

Recipe submitted by Yvonne M. Corrigan-Carr

WHO STOLE THE PIEROGI?

Makes a batch of 30 to 35

Ingredients:

6 cups flour
3 large eggs
3 Tbsp oil
½ tsp salt
¾ to <1 cup of milk (a full cup of liquid makes dough gluey)
¾ to <1 cup of water

1) Beat eggs and add oil and mix. Add salt and mix. Add flour. Slowly add half the milk and water as you blend in the flour. Keep adding milk and water until dough is just a little stiff and a little sticky. Let it rest in a bowl covered with a damp towel for at least 10 minutes.
2) Divide dough into manageable sizes and roll out very thin. Use a cookie cutter or glass to cut out circles about 3½ - 4 inches in diameter.
3) Fill with your choice of filling (See below*) and fold in half. Press the edges together with the tines of a fork to seal. Repeat.
4) Drop pierogi into a pot of boiling water. They will rise to the top when they're done.

5) Remove and place on a buttered cookie sheet to cool.

*Potato filling:
5 to 7 lbs of potatoes
12 – 16 oz of shredded farmer's cheese
¾ to 1 cup of minced onions
1 stick of butter
salt and pepper to taste

Boil potatoes until tender. Mash potatoes and mix all ingredients together. Let cool before using for filling.

*Sauerkraut filling:
1 – 27oz can of sauerkraut
1 – 10.5 oz can of beef gravy

Pour kraut in a colander. Rinse, rinse, rinse! Boil for 1 hour. Drain. For each can of kraut, mix in 1 can of gravy. Let cool before using for filling.

*Cheese filling:
1 lb farmers cheese
1 egg
3 tsp melted butter
3 tsp sugar

Mix all ingredients together.

Recipe submitted by Dianne Freeman

Soups
&
Stews

Notes

ANY NIGHT ALIBI CROCK POT STEW

Serves 4 to 6

Ingredients:

1 lb beef chuck or round cut in 1½" cubes
1 lb baby carrots or equivalent of regular size carrots
1 large yellow onion
4 medium size red potatoes
additional vegetables you like can be added
1 pkg Knorr Vegetable Soup
1Tbsp extra virgin olive oil
2 bay leaves

Additional if desired:
1 cube beef bouillon, dissolved in ½ cup of water
¼ cup sweet red wine
salt, pepper, garlic powder to taste
2 Tbsp flour

1) Place olive oil in bottom of crock-pot. Place meat cubes in olive oil and stir so the olive oil coats the meat. Turn on crock-pot to high.
2) Chop all vegetables into large "peasant style" sizes. Cut potatoes into quarters or smaller. Add to crock-pot.

3) Add Knorr Vegetable Soup mix. If desired, add beef bouillon, sweet wine, salt, pepper and garlic powder.
4) Mix all ingredients in pot together. Place the bay leaves on either side of the crock-pot.
5) Cover and cook 4 hours on high until done.
6) If desired, 30 minutes before finished, thicken broth with 2 Tbsp flour in ¼ cup water.

Serve with biscuits or corn bread.

This is also great the next day.

Recipe submitted by Michele D. Peters

BEWARE OF GREEKS BEARING LENTIL SOUP

Serves 6 to 12

Ingredients:

1 lb lentils
1 qt water
1 qt broth (chicken or beef)
2 medium onions, chopped
2 stalks celery, chopped
2 carrots, chopped
6 springs of parsley
3 garlic cloves, chopped
½ cup olive oil
½ can of tomato paste
2 bay leaves
1 Tbsp of ketchup
½ cup cooked tomatoes
1½ tsp crumbled oregano
3 Tbsp red wine vinegar

1) Soak lentils in water overnight.
2) Sauté vegetables in garlic and olive oil. Add to lentils along with parsley, tomato paste and bay leaves.

3) Bring to boil and simmer until lentils are tender (about ½ hour). During last 15 minutes of simmering, add oregano and cooked tomatoes.
4) Stir in red wine vinegar before serving.

May be used as an appetizer or main course. We make it as a main meal along with bread and a Greek salad.

Recipe submitted by Steven Schwartz

FRANKIE MacFARLANE'S LIME, LENTIL & GARBANZO SOUP

Serves 4

Ingredients:

1 cup lentils (any variety), rinsed
¼ cup rice (any variety white)
6 cups broth, divided (vegetable or chicken)
2 large onions, finely diced (or 1 large onion, plus
1 bunch of scallions, thinly sliced)
1 Tbsp vegetable oil
1¼ tsp salt
1 rounded tsp cumin
1 rounded tsp turmeric
6 garlic cloves, minced
1-15.5 oz can garbanzo beans, drained and rinsed
¼ cup unsweetened lime juice
½ cup chopped fresh parsley
1-2 Tbsp dried basil (optional)
toasted pita triangles, or pita chips

1) Bring 3 cups of broth to a boil in a soup pot.
2) Add lentils and rice. Reduce heat to low, cover, and simmer for 20 minutes, stirring occasionally.
3) In frying pan, sauté onions and garlic until tender. Add cumin, salt, turmeric, lime juice, and

garbanzos. Add 3 additional cups of broth and bring to boil.

4) Mix onion, broth, lime juice, garbanzo mixture into lentils.

5) Stir in parsley and basil.

Serve with pita chips.

I believe that food enriches the atmosphere and settings in the Frankie MacFarlane, Geologist, mysteries. In my fifth novel, Fracture, set in Tucson and the San Francisco Bay Area, Frankie makes lentil soup as comfort food after delivering tragic news to a supporting character.

Recipe submitted by Susan Cummins Miller

MALICIOUS MALLOW SOUP

Serves 8

Ingredients:

¼ stick salted butter (2 Tbsp)
½ medium sized sweet onion
1½ lbs new potatoes
1 lb fresh mallow leaves
6 tsp Better than Bouillon
6 cups water
¼ tsp fresh ground pepper
1 cup sour cream
1 garlic clove
12 oz canned or precooked chicken (optional)

1) In a six-quart pot, melt the butter on medium heat. Slice the onion and brown in butter but don't make the slices crispy.
2) Chop potatoes into small cubes. Wash the mallow leaves and cut into bite sized pieces.
3) Dissolve the bouillon in water and add to pot.
4) Slowly add the chopped potatoes and bring broth to a slow boil. Add the mallow leaves and bring to boil. Add pepper. Turn the heat down and simmer the covered soup for about 20 minutes until the potatoes and mallow leaves are soft.

5) Meanwhile, grate the garlic clove and mix into the sour cream in a separate bowl. Add salt to taste. If you use bouillon cubes you won't need extra salt.

Add canned or pre-cooked chicken, if desired.

Serve the soup with a tablespoon of the garlic flavored sour cream on top.
It stores well in the refrigerator and tastes better when reheated.

I give my guests a tiny sample of the soup to make sure they know they will like it before serving the bowls. Most people eating mallow soup for the first time want seconds.
If you can't find mallow in your grocery store, you might find it growing in your back yard. If you pick your own, make sure it has not been sprayed with any herbicide.

Recipe submitted by Robert Dukelow

RIBOLLITA GONE ROGUE

Serves 4

Ingredients:

4 oz pancetta, chopped
¼ cup olive oil
1 onion, chopped
1 or 2 carrots, chopped
1 celery stalk, chopped
1 zucchini, chopped
3 cloves garlic, minced
2 cups (15-oz can) diced tomatoes (or peeled Roma
    tomatoes diced)
2 Tbsp of tomato paste
2 cups (15-oz can) of cannellini beans, drained
1 lb bunch of kale (alt: spinach or cabbage)
4 cups chicken broth
salt to taste (*Tuscans don't use much salt in this dish*)
black pepper
red pepper flakes
Herbs de Provence or basil.
ciabatta rolls (or toasted thick slices of whole grain or
    sourdough bread)
Parmesan cheese, shaved

1) Place 2 Tbsp olive oil in a large pot over medium

heat. Add pancetta and onion. Sauté for 10 minutes until the onion is translucent. (Cook pancetta first if you like it crisp.)

2) Add the carrots, garlic, celery, red pepper flakes, salt and pepper. Keep heat at medium-low and continue to cook for 7 to 10 minutes.

3) Add the tomatoes, tomato paste, zucchini, kale (or cabbage), basil or Herbs de Provence. Cook for another 10 minutes over medium-low heat.

4) Add to the pot drained cannellini beans and 4 cups of chicken broth. Bring to boil, and then reduce to simmer for 30 minutes and let the flavors come alive.

5) Now comes the bread. One choice is to cut the bread into cubes or break into small pieces and add to the stew. Simmer for 10 more minutes.

Serve topped with Parmesan cheese.

You could choose to slice a ciabatta roll in half, sprinkle with olive oil and put under a broiler until brown. Then place at the bottom of a dish and ladle stew over top. Sprinkle with cheese and serve.

This is a farmer's stew from the Italian Tuscan region. In The Yemen Contract I served this dish to two of my main characters in a restaurant in Florence. When a cook decides to prepare this dish, he/she goes to the cupboard or outside in the garden and gathers vegetables that look good that day. Which vegetables they use depends upon the recipe passed down for generations in the family.

Recipe submitted by Arthur Kerns

VICTIMLESS VEGETABLE STEW – Vegetarian

Serves 4 to 6

Ingredients:

2 Tbsp butter
6 mushrooms, diced
1 Tbsp extra virgin olive oil
1 big or 3 small leeks
1 shallot or small onion
1 carrot, peeled and chopped
3 Yukon gold potatoes
7 cups vegetable broth (e.g. Imagine Foods)
¼ cup steel cut oats
1½ tsp parsley, dried
1 tsp Herbs de Provence or thyme
1 tsp fresh black pepper
salt & pepper to taste
2 tomatoes

1) Dice all vegetables excluding the mushrooms. Slice the mushrooms into bite-sized pieces.
2) In a soup pot melt the butter. Add the mushrooms and cook until golden brown.
3) Add the oil to the pot. Toss leeks, onion and a few of the carrots into mushrooms and continue to sauté until the onions caramelize.

4) Deglaze pot with a small amount of broth and scrape the bottom. Add 2 more cups of the broth
5) Add the rest of carrots and all of the potatoes. Cover the vegetables with the remaining broth. Add oats and herbs.
6) Bring to a simmer, cover, and allow to cook for 25 minutes, or until the vegetables are tender.

Recipe submitted by Sharon Lynn

Salads
&
Sandwiches

Notes

A LITTLE SPINACH WON'T KILL YA

Ingredients:

Quinoa:
1 cup uncooked white quinoa
1 tsp cumin seeds
1 tsp fennel seeds
1¾ cups water
½ tsp sea salt

Salad:
3 cups baby spinach
1 cup cooked chickpeas, drained and rinsed
1 cup chopped, pitted dates
⅓ cup toasted pistachio nuts, coarsely chopped
4 to 5 Tbsp sumac powder (do not skip this ingredient!)

Dressing:
2 Tbsp extra-virgin olive oil
3 Tbsp lemon juice
½ tsp ground coriander
½ tsp sea salt
ground pepper to taste

1) Place rinsed, drained quinoa in an ungreased, medium-sized pot and toast over medium heat

for 3 minutes until grains are dry and lightly toasted. Some quinoa grains will pop. Add the cumin and fennel seeds. Toast another minute. Add water and salt and bring to a rolling boil. Stir a couple of times and then cover the pot with a fitted lid. Reduce to low heat and cook for approximately 20 minutes. All the water should be absorbed and the grains tender. Use a fork to loosen up and fluff quinoa, re-cover the pot, remove from heat, and allow to cool for 5 minutes.

2) While the quinoa cooks, combine the spinach, chickpeas, dates, and pistachios in a mixing bowl. If you are chopping the dates yourself, use a sharp knife and dip the blade frequently in cold water to prevent sticking.

3) Prepare the dressing by whisking together all the ingredients in a large liquid measuring cup. Pour the dressing over salad ingredients and toss to coat completely.

4) After the quinoa has cooled a little, transfer it to the mixing bowl with the salad ingredients and add the sumac. Toss everything together.

Serve warm or at room temperature via a large serving bowl or divide among four plates.

This dish is Vegan, Gluten-Free Friendly. Date bits coated in oat flour are an easy option but might not be gluten-free.

Recipe submitted by Denise Ganley

G-MEN'S GERMAN POTATO SALAD

Ingredients:

Salad:
10 – 12 red potatoes, boiled and diced
4 hardboiled eggs, chopped
4 stalks of celery, chopped
Add onion (if desired)

Hot bacon dressing:
4 slices bacon, fried and cut into bits; do not drain bacon
    drippings
¾ cup red wine vinegar
¾ cup sugar
2 eggs

1) Mix together all ingredients for salad and set
   aside.
2) Mix together red wine vinegar and sugar.
3) Beat eggs with a fork and add to vinegar and
   sugar mixture.
4) Add the mixture to the bacon and reheat, stirring
   constantly until thickened.
5) Pour the dressing over the salad and mix
   together.
Can be served hot or cold.

Recipe submitted by Suzanne Flaig

Notes

UP NORTH FRENCH CONNECTION POTATO SALAD

Serves 8 to 10

Ingredients:

1 lb sliced bacon
1 lb Polish sausage
3 lbs small red potatoes, sliced ¼" thick
1 lb fresh or frozen green beans or broccoli

1) Cut bacon in 1½" strips; they will separate while they cook. Cook over medium heat about 15 minutes, until lightly browned, stirring occasionally. Drain grease off.
2) Remove casing from sausage and cut in 1½ inch rounds.
3) Place sliced potatoes in salted boiling water and cook 8 to 10 minutes until fork tender. Drain.
4) Wash and trim green beans or broccoli. Cut into 2 to 3" pieces. Place in another saucepan with ½ inch boiling salted water. Cook about 10 minutes until tender-crisp.

Dressing:
½ cup olive oil or salad dressing

¼ cup tarragon vinegar
¼ cup beef bouillon
½ cup scallions, chopped
¼ cup fresh parsley (can use dried)
1 garlic clove, crushed
1 tsp salt
⅛ cup sugar (optional)
1 tsp. dry mustard
½ tsp. basil
½ tsp. tarragon
pepper to taste

1) Combine all dressing ingredients and mix well.
2) In large bowl, combine potatoes and beans.
3) Add bacon and sausage.
4) Pour dressing over entire mixture. Marinate at least 2 to 3 hours.
5) Heat through before serving.

Recipe submitted by Patricia Curren

SHAW'S FAVORITE MEATLOAF SANDWICH

Ingredients:

2 thick slices of leftover meatloaf
2 pieces of white bread
2 slices of red onion
mustard and ketchup to taste

1) Assemble sandwich thus: On one slice of bread, spread 1 or 2 Tbsp of yellow mustard. Arrange slabs of meatloaf on top of mustard.
2) Press the onion into the meatloaf so it won't fall off. Pour two or three glugs of ketchup over all. Top with final slice of bread, pressing it down firmly with the heel of your hand to glue into place.

For best results, eat over a bucket to catch the drips.

Recipe Submitted by Donis Casey

Notes

SUSPECTED STATISTICIAN'S SALAD SANDWICH

Serves 4 to 6

Ingredients:

1 cup tofu (or ground chicken)
½ cup water (reconstitutes tofu)
1 Tbsp grated ginger
2 cloves garlic, minced
2 Tbsp Bragg Liquid Aminos (or soy sauce)
4 scallions, minced
½ lb mushrooms, minced
¼ tsp red pepper
8 oz jar plum sauce
lettuce leaves

1) Mix the tofu and water to reconstitute the tofu. Add the rest of the ingredients and mix well.
2) Sauté until the tofu is cooked.
3) Serve in a lettuce leaf with plum sauce

Recipe submitted by Kwinn Mitchell

Notes

Vegetable Dishes

Notes

SILENCE OF THE STUFFED YAMS

Serves 4

Preheat oven to 400°

Ingredients:
4 garnet yams
2 Tbsp olive oil
1 shallot, diced
1 garlic clove, minced
1 (4-inch) sprig fresh rosemary
¼ tsp red pepper flakes
1 can drained white beans (Cannellini or Great
   Northern)
2 bunches of kale, trimmed and sliced into ribbons
juice of ¼ lemon
salt and freshly ground black pepper

1) Scrub the yams and prick them in a few places with a fork. Place them on a baking sheet and bake at 400° until soft all the way through, about 45 minutes to 1 hour.
2) Rinse 2 bunches of kale and remove leaves from stems. Drain well. Slice the leaves into ribbons about ¼" to ½" wide. In a large bowl, sprinkle kale with about 1 tsp of sea salt. Massage with your bare hands. After a few minutes, the kale will feel soft and it will shrink in volume

considerably. Massaging makes it easier to chew and digest.

3) About 15 minutes before the yams are done, heat the olive oil over low-medium heat. Add the shallots and cook until softened, about 5 minutes.

4) Add the garlic, rosemary sprig, and red pepper flakes and cook, stirring, for about a minute.

5) Add the beans and cook for 5 minutes, stirring occasionally.

6) Add the kale, cover the pan, and cook, stirring occasionally, for about 5 minutes until the flavors blend.

7) Remove the rosemary sprig, stir in the lemon juice, and season to taste with salt and pepper.

To serve, slice each yam lengthwise and push on the ends to open up the middle. Spoon the beans and greens into the center.

You can use sweet potatoes instead of garnet yams, but I like the bright orange color contrasted with the green kale.

Recipe submitted by Kathy McIntosh

STUFFED SQUASH BLOSSOMS SCAM

Preheat oven to 350°

Ingredients:

stuffing recipe of your choice
squash blossoms

1) Precook your favorite stuffing recipe.
2) Calculate quantity of stuffing based on the size and quantity of blossoms. For small blossoms, use a tablespoon or two. For large blossoms, use as much as for a large mushroom cap.
3) Cool stuffing to room temperature. Rinse the squash blossoms and lay them on a paper towel to dry.
4) Stuff each blossom according to its size. If you use a cheesy stuffing, stuff only 3/4 full and twist the open ends closed before baking.
5) Bake at 350° in a preheated oven until blossoms are hot, about 10 minutes.

I have never shopped for squash blossoms because we had a huge garden in Ohio. However, friends tell me squash blossoms are available at farmers' markets and probably through "the source-of-everything"—Amazon. I've served stuffed squash blossoms as a luncheon entrée and appetizer using the same stuffing as for stuffed mushrooms. The dessert stuffing just takes a little ingenuity, such mixing ground graham crackers with ground nuts flavored with honey. Be daring—add some cinnamon. My inner chef experiments with spices, herbs, and flavorings of all kinds.

Recipe submitted by Elizabeth Remic Kral

Desserts

Notes

Cakes

Notes

_____
_____
_____
_____
_____
_____
_____
_____
_____
_____
_____
_____
_____
_____
_____
_____
_____
_____
_____
_____
_____
_____
_____
_____
_____
_____
_____
_____
_____
_____
_____

AMARETTO SWOON CHEESECAKE CAPER

Serves 9

Preheat oven to 350°

Ingredients:

1 cup graham cracker crumbs
½ cup almonds, toasted and ground
¼ cup (half stick) butter, melted
⅓ cup + 2 Tbsp sugar
⅓ cup + 4 Tbsp Amaretto
4 oz almond paste
2 Tbsp flour
24 oz cream cheese (3 x 8-oz packages)
4 large eggs
1 cup sour cream
¼ cup sliced almonds

Grease a 9" spring-form pan.

1) Allow the cream cheese to soften at room temperature.
2) Combine graham cracker crumbs, ground almonds, butter, 1 Tbsp sugar, and 1 Tbsp Amaretto.

3) Press crust mixture on bottom of spring-form pan and up the sides of the pan. Refrigerate crust until cold.

4) Combine almond paste, ⅓ cup sugar, and flour. Beat until smooth. Add ⅓ cup Amaretto and beat. Add softened cream cheese, one package at a time, and beat in. Add one egg at a time and beat. Beat well until smooth. Pour batter into chilled crust. Bake 45-50 minutes at 350°. Cheesecake will not be fully set in center.

5) While cheesecake bakes, blend together sour cream, 3 Tbsp Amaretto, and 1 Tbsp sugar. Spread mixture over baked cheesecake.

6) Return to oven for 20 minutes or until center is firm.

7) Cool at room temperature on rack for one hour, then refrigerate in pan for four hours.

To serve, remove sides of spring-form pan and garnish with sliced almonds.

Recipe submitted by Kris Neri

CAMILLA'S COFFEE WALNUT CAKE

Serves 8

Preheat oven to 350°

Ingredients:

The Layer Cake:
1 cup shelled walnuts, divided into 2 containers.
1 scant cup sugar (Camilla uses ¾ organic cane sugar,
   which has a pale brown color, and ¼ regular white
   cane sugar.) Remove 1 Tbsp sugar and reserve.
1 Tbsp instant espresso coffee.
1⅓ cups all-purpose flour
2 tsp fresh baking powder
½ tsp ground cinnamon
¼ tsp baking soda
¼ tsp salt
10 Tbsp (1¼ sticks) unsalted butter, room temperature
3 large eggs and 1 egg yolk, room temperature
½ tsp vanilla extract
¾ cup buttermilk

The Frosting (Icing):
4½ tsp instant espresso powder dissolved in 1 Tbsp
water
12 oz chilled heavy whipping cream

½ cup (4 oz) crème fraiche **or** 3½ oz cream cheese softened with 3 Tbsp sour cream or whole milk yogurt.
½ cup powdered sugar
½ tsp vanilla extract

The Topping:
3 oz walnuts, chopped fine
¼ tsp ground cinnamon
tiny pinch of salt

1) Butter and flour three 8½" pans (the cheap aluminum pans from the supermarket do just fine) or use two 9" pans with sides that are 1½" high.
2) In the blender or food processor, grate ½ cup walnuts, 1 Tbsp sugar, and espresso powder until the nuts are finely ground.
3) Whisk the flour, baking powder, cinnamon, baking soda and salt in a medium bowl to blend. Whisking the flour mixture is important as it aerates it, creating a lighter crumb.
4) In a large bowl, beat the butter until smooth. Gradually add remaining sugar (1 cup minus 1 Tbsp) and beat until fluffy. Beat in the eggs, one at a time, then the egg yolk.
5) Add the walnut mixture and vanilla. Mix into the batter. Reduce the mixer speed to low, and add the flour and the buttermilk alternately, starting and ending with the flour. Fold in the remaining ½ cup of chopped walnuts and stir.
6) Divide equally among the pans and place in the oven. Bake at 350° for 25-26 minutes or until a skewer comes out clean.

7) Remove the cakes from the oven, let cool in the pans for five minutes, then turn onto racks and cool completely.

Frosting:

1) When the cakes are cool, stir the espresso mixed with water in a large bowl. Add the crème fraiche **or** cream cheese/yogurt/sour cream mix. Add sugar, vanilla and cream.
2) Beat until the filling is thick and forms swirls.
3) Place the first cake layer, flat side up on a plate. Spread filling over the cake. Place the second layer, also upside down, on top, and again spread the filling over it. Place the last layer topside up, and frost.
4) You should have enough left over to ice the entire cake around the sides as well.

Topping:

Mix the walnuts, cinnamon and salt and sprinkle over the top of the cake. OR you could simply place up to a dozen walnuts in a circle round the top of the cake.
Cover with a cake dome and chill for at least an hour or overnight.

This recipe appears in my book, Lipstick on the Strawberry. The title refers to a food-stylist's trick of coloring an unripe strawberry to make it look good for a photograph. It's a metaphor for what my protagonist, caterer Camilla Fetherwell, finds when she goes home for her ultra-respectable father's funeral and finds things are not at all what they seem on the surface. In my story,

Camilla brings this cake to the woman she thinks will confirm her suspicions about a family mystery. Instead, she gets a shock.

Recipe Submitted by Margaret Ann Spence

CORRUPTIVE COCA-COLA CAKE

Serves 12

Preheat oven to 350°

Ingredients:

2 cups all-purpose flour
2 cups sugar
½ tsp salt
1 tsp baking soda
½ tsp cinnamon
1 cup butter
¼ cup unsweetened cocoa powder
1 cup Coca-Cola
½ cup buttermilk
2 eggs
1 tsp vanilla extract
½ tsp coffee extract (optional)

1) Mix the flour, 2 cups sugar, salt, baking soda, and cinnamon. Set aside.
2) Mix in a saucepan over medium heat: the butter, unsweetened cocoa powder, Coca-Cola, and buttermilk. Bring to a boil, stirring constantly. Once it reaches a vigorous, rolling boil, remove

from heat and add to flour mixture. Use a whisk to stir.

3) Add eggs, vanilla extract, coffee extract (optional).
4) Pour batter into a greased 9x13 oblong pan. Bake 30 minutes at 350°. *DO NOT OVERBAKE.* Cake is done when toothpick is inserted and comes out clean.

Ten minutes before cake is done, mix ingredients for glaze in a saucepan.

Glaze:
½ cup butter
¼ cup unsweetened cocoa powder
4 cups confectioner's sugar (10x, doesn't need sifting)
½ cup Coca-Cola
1 cup chopped pecans

1) Mix together: butter, unsweetened cocoa powder, confectioner's sugar, and Coca-Cola. Bring to a boil. Once it reaches a boil, slowly stir in the pecans.
2) Use a skewer or slender knife to poke holes every 3" or so in cake. Pour glaze over top of warm cake and let sit five minutes.

Serve warm with vanilla ice cream or alone.

Recipe submitted by Debra S. Sanders

CRIME SCENE CAKES

Serves 6

Preheat oven to 425°

Ingredients:

coconut oil cooking spray
2 Tbsp granulated sugar, (plus 4 Tbsp more for dusting
   the muffin tin)
6 oz semisweet chocolate
6 Tbsp unrefined coconut oil
⅓ cup all-purpose flour
pinch of fine salt
2 large eggs plus 2 large egg yolks
2½ tsp red gel food coloring
3 oz cream cheese, at room temperature
2 tsp vanilla extract
powdered sugar for dusting

1) Spray 6 cups of a standard muffin tin with
   the coconut oil cooking spray, sprinkle with
   granulated sugar to cover the entire cup
   and dust off any excess to prevent sticking.
   Set aside.

2) Melt the chocolate and coconut oil together in a double boiler for 5 to 7 minutes. Remove from the heat, add the flour and salt and stir until combined. Whisk the eggs and egg yolks together in a small bowl and slowly add to the chocolate mixture. Stir in 1 tsp of the red food coloring.
3) In a small bowl, beat together the cream cheese, granulated sugar, vanilla extract and remaining 1½ tsp of red food coloring. Spoon the filling mixture into a disposable pastry or icing bag and make a small cut when ready to fill.
4) Using a heaping ¼ cup scoop, divide the lava cake mixture among the prepared muffin cups. Fill the centers with about 1½ Tbsp of the cream cheese mixture.
5) Bake at 425° until the edges are firm but the centers are not set, 9 to 11 minutes.
6) Cool for 2 to 3 minutes, invert and sprinkle with powdered sugar.

Serve immediately.

Recipe submitted by Jess Lourey

GRAND THEFT MARNIER BUNDT CAKE

Serves 10 to 12

Preheat oven to 350°

Ingredients:

Cake:
2¼ cups all-purpose flour: more for the pan
2 cups light brown sugar*
1½ teaspoons baking powder
½ teaspoon baking soda
6 oz (12 tsp) unsalted butter, softened; more for the
   pan
¾ cup canola, grape seed or other mild flavored oil
1½ Tbsp grated lemon zest
1 Tbsp grated orange zest
1 Tbsp vanilla extract
½ cup fresh orange juice, strained
5 large eggs

1) Butter and flour a 10" tube pan or 12 cup Bundt
   pan (my choice).
2) Sift the flour, sugar, baking powder and soda into
   the large bowl of a stand mixer fitted with a
   paddle attachment.

3) Add the butter and mix on low speed until fine crumbs form. Change to the whisk attachment. With the machine running on medium speed, whisk in the oil, lemon zest, orange zest, vanilla extract and orange juice.
4) Add eggs one at a time then increase the speed to high whisking the batter until light (about 3 minutes), scraping the sides of the bowl if necessary.
5) Pour the batter into the prepared pan and bake at 350° until a toothpick inserted in the cake comes out clean (45 to 50 minutes).

Syrup and Glaze:
⅓ cup frozen orange juice concentrate, thawed
1 Tbsp unsalted butter, melted
2 Tbsp Grand Marnier
¼ cup confectioner's sugar

1) While the cake bakes, whisk together the orange juice concentrate, butter, Grand Marnier and the confectioner's sugar in a small bowl.
2) When the cake is done, set the pan on a rack to cool for 5 minutes.
3) With a thin wooden skewer, poke the cake all the way through to the bottom of the pan up to 100 places. Pour ⅓ cup of the syrup over the cake and let stand for 1 hour before removing the cake from the pan. (I like to wrap the cake in plastic wrap and keep it up to 3 days at room temperature. It improves the flavor).
4) Save the remaining syrup in a small glass jar at room temperature.

5) When serving, stir the remaining syrup. Set the cake on a rack and pour the glaze over it. Wait about 10 minutes and then slice and serve.

You can substitute Splenda mix or Stevia for the sugar. I sometimes substitute Limoncello (homemade) for the Grand Marnier. You could also use Cointreau or Triple Sec in a pinch.

Recipe submitted by Howard (Doc) Carron

Notes

HITMAN'S HOT BUTTERED RUM CAKE

Serves 10 to 12

Preheat oven to 350°

Prepare pan:
Butter-flavored Crisco
1½ cups crushed pecans

1) Coat interior of Bundt pan well with Butter-flavored Crisco, so it's completely covered and smooth. Line pan with crushed pecans.

Cake:
1 package Duncan Hines Butter Recipe Cake Mix
3 large eggs
½ cup melted butter (or vegetable oil)
½ cup water
½ cup Bacardi white rum
1 small package Jell-O *Instant* Vanilla Pudding Mix
crushed pecans

1) Beat cake mix, eggs, oil, water, rum and pudding mix on low speed 1 minute, until ingredients are moistened. Beat 2 minutes on medium speed, scraping bowl often, until smooth.

2) Pour batter into prepared Bundt Pan. Sprinkle pecans on top if desired.
3) Bake 50 minutes. Check cake 5 minutes before end of baking time to avoid over baking. Cake is done when tester or toothpick inserted into center comes out clean.
4) Remove cake from oven. Leave cake in pan and set aside.

Hot Buttered Rum Topping:
½ cup (1 stick) butter
1 cup white sugar
¼ cup water
¼ cup Captain Morgan's Spiced Rum
¼ tsp cinnamon
¼ tsp cardamom
⅛ tsp allspice

1) Melt butter in saucepan. Add sugar, cinnamon, cardamom, allspice, water and rum. Stir over medium heat until mixture is smooth and reaches a rolling boil. Boil two minutes, stirring constantly.
2) Pour rum mixture over cake, very slowly and evenly.
3) Using a knife, gently pull sides of cake from pan so liquid goes to bottom of pan. Liquid should surround cake.
4) Let sit 5-10 minutes until moisture is completely absorbed before turning onto a plate. Cool before serving. Serve alone or with whipped cream garnish.

Recipe submitted by Yvonne M. Corrigan-Carr

LAW-ABIDING CHOCOLATE CAKE

Preheat oven to 350°

Ingredients:

Cake:
1 cup white sugar
1 Tbsp butter
1 egg yolk
½ cup sour milk (*substitute:* buttermilk)*
½ tsp baking soda
¼ tsp salt
1 tsp vanilla
3 heaping tsp cocoa
½ cup hot water
1½ cups flour
1 tsp baking powder

1) Cream 1 cup white sugar and 1 level Tbsp of soft butter together. Add the yolk of 1 egg and stir. Add ½ cup of sour milk (*substitute:* buttermilk)*, ½ level tsp baking soda, ¼ tsp salt and 1 tsp of vanilla.

2) In a separate container dissolve 3 heaping tsp of cocoa in ½ cup of hot water. Add 1½ cups of sifted flour, into which sift 1 rounded tsp of baking powder

3) Combine all the ingredients. Bake in a loaf pan at 350° for about 45 minutes.

Frosting:
1 egg white
salt
1 tsp lemon juice
1 tsp confectioner's sugar

1) Beat the white of 1 egg. Add a pinch of salt and 1 tsp each of lemon juice and confectioner's sugar.
2) Spread on the cooled cake.

My mother grew up in a farming community near Syracuse, NY. The farm women tended to share recipes. I understand that the above recipe was handed down from my great-grandmother. At the time they were using wood fired stoves and, when available, ice to cool ingredients. I have no idea what 'cook in a moderate oven' translates into. When I was six, we visited a great-aunt who was 99 years old. For the occasion, she baked chocolate cake and we drank fresh milk gathered from one of her cows. The original recipe probably was written down in the 1890s and is described as simple and inexpensive and very good.

The original recipe calls for sour milk. Since it is hard to find in stores, the editors suggest using buttermilk in its place.

Recipe submitted by Bill Butler

ORANGE MUFFINS OF MENTAL CRUELTY

Serves 4 to 8

Preheat oven to 375°

Ingredients:

1¼ cup flour
2 tsp baking powder
½ tsp salt
¼ tsp cinnamon, ground
1 Tbsp sugar
1 Tbsp orange rind, grated
1 cup orange juice
2 eggs, separated

1) Mix together the flour, baking powder, salt, cinnamon, sugar, and orange rind.
2) Combine orange juice and egg yolks. Add to dry ingredients. Batter will be lumpy.
3) Beat egg whites until stiff. Fold in to batter.
4) Pour into muffin tin and bake at 375° until golden, approximately 20 minutes.

Recipe submitted by Kwinn Mitchell

Notes

SASHA'S SINFUL DARK CHOCOLATE MATCHA BALLS

Makes 12 matcha balls

Ingredients:

1 cup almonds (or substitute cashews, walnuts, or other
  nuts)
1 cup pitted dates tightly packed (or substitute raisins)
1 tsp matcha green tea powder
pinch of salt
1-12 oz pkg of dark chocolate, melted
shredded coconut (optional)

1) Put the almonds in a high-speed blender or food
   processor until mealy.
2) Remove almond meal and put dates or raisins
   into the processor. Pulse until they form a ball.
3) Add the almond meal back in. Then, add the
   matcha, salt, and pulse until mixed well.
4) Melt the dark chocolate wedges until they are a
   smooth liquid.
5) Remove the blend from the processor and form
   into small balls by rolling between your palms.
6) Dip the balls into the dark chocolate and place
   them on a cookie pan covered with a baking

sheet. Sprinkle the shredded coconut on top, if desired.

7) Refrigerate for at least two hours before devouring.

This recipe is inspired by the romantic suspense series Fever: A Ballroom Romance, by Tonya Plank. Sasha, an amateur cook and dance partner to his beloved Rory, delights in making delicious concoctions for Rory. These matcha balls, packed with antioxidants, carbs, and protein, and drizzled in sinful Godiva dark chocolate, are small enough for Rory to pop in her mouth for a luscious last-minute energy boost before hitting the grueling, trap-laden competition dance floor.

Recipe submitted by Tonya Plank

STICKY-FINGERED FRUIT COCKTAIL CAKE

Serves 10 to 12

Preheat oven to 350°

Ingredients:

1½ cups sugar
2 cups of all-purpose flour
2 tsp baking soda
2 tsp salt
2 cups or 1 – 16 to 17 oz can of fruit cocktail
2 eggs
1 tsp vanilla (you may substitute spices such as cinnamon, nutmeg, a pinch of clove for vanilla)
½ cup brown sugar
½ cup nuts

1) Mix the first *seven* ingredients in order and pour into a 13" by 9" baking pan.
2) Before baking, sprinkle the top with ½ cup of brown sugar and ½ cup of nuts (we always use pecans), or after baking you may ice the cake with German chocolate icing.
3) Bake for 45 minutes at 350°, until a toothpick inserted in the center comes out clean.

This very easy cake is my mother's recipe and is famous in my family for its utter deliciousness. The longer it sits the more scrumptious it becomes. After two or three days it will make you burst into tears of joy. I have never used it in a novel.

Recipe submitted by Donis Casey

THE DARKNESS WITHIN GUINNESS CHOCOLATE CAKE

Serves 8 to 10

Preheat oven to 350°

Ingredients:

Cake:
1 cup Guinness (or other dark stout)
½ cup butter, cubed
2 cups sugar
¾ cup baking cocoa
2 large eggs, beaten
⅔ cup sour cream
3 tsp vanilla extract
2 cups all-purpose flour
1½ tsp baking soda
1 tsp cinnamon

Frosting:
8 oz package cream cheese, softened
1½ cups confectioners' sugar
½ cup heavy whipping cream

1) Grease a 9" springform cake pan and line the bottom with parchment paper; set aside.

2) In a small saucepan, heat beer and butter until butter is melted. Remove from the heat. Whisk in sugar, cinnamon and cocoa until blended.
3) Combine the eggs, sour cream and vanilla and whisk into beer mixture.
4) Combine flour and baking soda; whisk into beer mixture until smooth. Pour batter into prepared pan.
5) Bake at 350° for 45-50 minutes or until a toothpick inserted in the center comes out clean. Cool completely in pan on a wire rack. Remove sides of pan.
6) In a large bowl, beat cream cheese until fluffy. Add confectioners' sugar and cream; beat until smooth (do not over-beat).
7) Remove cake from the pan and place on a platter or cake stand. Ice top of cake with frosting and sprinkle very lightly with a mixture of cinnamon and cocoa powder.

Refrigerate any leftovers.

This dessert is perfect to enjoy on a dark and stormy evening with an after-dinner cup of coffee or an Irish cream liqueur. Guests may kill to get this recipe from you. It is that good.

Recipe submitted by Erynn Crowley

WOODCHIPPER CHOPPED APPLE CAKE

Serves up to 12

Preheat oven to 350°

Ingredients:

2 cups brown sugar
2 large eggs
½ cup vegetable oil
2 cups flour
2 tsp soda
2 tsp cinnamon
1 tsp salt
1 tsp nutmeg
4 cups chopped apples
½ cup chopped walnuts (optional)

1) Mix brown sugar, eggs and vegetable oil together in a large bowl.
2) Combine flour, soda, cinnamon, salt and nutmeg.
3) Stir flour mixture into sugar-egg liquid. Batter will be very stiff.
4) Add chopped apples and walnuts.
5) Spread batter in 9" x 13" greased and floured baking pan.
6) Bake one hour at 350°.

<u>Buttercream Frosting</u>:
3 cups powdered sugar
½ cup salted butter, softened
1½ tsp real vanilla extract
1 – 2 Tbsp half & half
chopped walnuts

1) Combine powdered sugar with butter, vanilla extract and half & half.
2) Add additional milk or powdered sugar to reach a smooth, spreadable frosting
3) Garnish with additional chopped walnuts.

Recipe submitted by R K Olson

Cookies & Bars

Notes

CRIMINALLY HOT CHOCO-CAYENNE HOLIDAY COOKIES

Makes 20 cookies

Preheat oven to 350°

Ingredients:

3 cups powdered sugar
¾ cup unsweetened cocoa powder
1 Tbsp cornstarch
¼ tsp salt
½ tsp cayenne pepper
2 large egg–whites
1 large egg–whole
1 tsp vanilla extract
½ cup chocolate chips**
parchment paper, baking quality

1) In large bowl, stir the powdered sugar, cocoa powder, cornstarch, salt and cayenne pepper together until evenly combined.
2) Add the egg whites, whole egg and vanilla to the powdered sugar mixture.
3) Carefully stir the mixture until all of the powdered sugar has dissolved into the eggs and a very thick batter forms. Keep stirring until it

eventually melts in. The mixture will be very thick and stiff so use a strong spoon. **If desired, add the chocolate chips and stir until incorporated.

4) Line 2 baking sheets with parchment paper. Spoon the batter one heaping tablespoon at a time, aiming for 10 cookies per sheet. Be sure to leave a couple of inches between each cookie because they will spread.

5) Bake at 350° for 14 minutes. Cookies should be puffed and cracked.

6) Allow cookies to cool before removing from the parchment paper.

*This cookie is not only sweet and spicy, it's also gluten free. **The cookie is spicier and (in my opinion) more attractive without the chips but omitting them may reduce the quantity of cookies produced.*

Recipe submitted by Connie Flynn

GRIFTER GRANDMA'S DATE BARS

Makes 12 to 15 bars

Preheat oven to 350°

Ingredients:

1½ cups quick oatmeal
¾ cup butter or margarine
½ tsp baking soda
1½ cups flour
1 cup brown or white sugar
¼ tsp salt
¾ lbs chopped dates
½ cup water
½ cup white sugar
pinch of salt

1) Combine oatmeal, baking soda, salt, flour and brown or white sugar.
2) Cut in the butter as for a piecrust.
3) Press half the oatmeal mixture into a greased 9" x 13" pan.
4) Cook dates, water, white sugar and salt until thick.
5) Cool date mixture and spread on crust without touching edge.

6) Lightly press the rest of the crumb mixture on top all the way to the edge.
7) Bake 25 to 30 minutes at 350° until lightly browned.
8) Cut into squares when cooled.

Recipe submitted by Patricia Curren

LEMON SCREAM COOKIES

Makes 24 large cookies

Preheat oven to 350°

Ingredients:

1 roll of refrigerated sugar cookie dough
3 oz cream cheese
½ cup all-purpose flour
5 tsp grated lemon peel
1½ cup powdered sugar
3 Tbsp lemon juice

1) Let dough stand at room temperature to soften.
2) In large bowl, break up cookie dough. Add cream cheese, flour and 3 tsp of the lemon peel. Stir until well blended.
3) Roll dough in 1-inch balls and place about 2 inches apart on cookie sheets. (For larger cookies, use 1½ inch balls of dough.)
4) Bake at 350° for 12 to 14 minutes or until edges are golden brown. Cool completely on cooling racks about 20 minutes.

5) In medium bowl, stir powdered sugar and lemon juice until smooth. Frost cookies and sprinkle with remaining lemon peel.

Recipe submitted by Nicolette Lemmon

LOADED CANNON BALLS

Ingredients:

1 pkg dark chocolate Oreo Cookies
½ cup rum
1 cup powdered sugar on a paper plate

1) Put cookies into a gallon sized Ziploc bag.
2) Close tight and crush with a mallet or use your fist.
3) Add rum and massage the bag until absorbed and thick.
4) Roll into two or three-inch balls.
5) Roll balls in powdered sugar.
6) Stack on a plate.

I like to make a small flag with the note: Loaded and ready to fire! Quick and good for adult parties

Recipe submitted by RP Dahlke

Notes

MRS. MOORE'S POLISH HANG 'EM HIGH, BOWTIE COOKIES

Ingredients:

6 eggs
1 Tbsp sugar
½ cup unsalted butter, melted
½ tsp salt
1 tsp vanilla
2 oz rum
1 cup cream
3 cups flour
vegetable oil for frying
powdered sugar

1) Beat eggs in bowl of electric stand mixer using whisk attachment. Gradually add sugar, butter, salt and vanilla, beating until light and fluffy. Add rum and cream, and continue beating until mixture is thick and well incorporated.
2) With dough hook, mix in flour in small amounts, about ½ cup at a time, until well combined and dough is elastic.
3) Divide dough into four balls. On a floured surface, give dough ball a few good whacks with the rolling pin then knead dough for about 3

minutes. Use rolling pin to roll out dough into a thin, long rectangle shape. Roll ⅛ inch or less.

4) Use a rolling pizza cutter, cut dough into 1½ - inch wide strips. On the diagonal, cut dough to make pieces about 3½ inches long.

5) With a sharp knife, cut a small slit, about ¾ of an inch, in the center of each strip. Lift each piece and tuck one end into the slit of the cookie and pull it through to form a bowtie. Let dough gently dangle for a couple of seconds to elongate and shape the cookie.

6) Use a large pot to heat oil until hot. Test temperature with a small piece of dough. It should sink to the bottom, then immediately rise to the surface and begin to blister.

7) Fry cookies in small batches, 5 or 6 at a time. Use tongs to flip cookies once. They are done when they are golden and blistered, not brown.

8) Cool on a baking sheet lined with paper towels. When cool and dry, dust with powdered sugar.

Recipe submitted by Timothy W. Moore

PUT 'EM BEHIND GRANOLA BARS

Ingredients:

2½ cups granola
4 cups marshmallows
¼ cup butter or similar spread
½ cup peanuts
½ cup hazelnuts
½ cup cashews
1 cup dried apricots (smaller the better)
1 cup dried strawberries
1 cup banana flakes
1 cup dried mango (<½ inch pieces)
1 cup dried orange flavored cranberries

1) Slowly melt butter and marshmallows in a 3 quart or larger pot at low heat until syrupy.
2) Remove from heat. Combine granola, nuts, and seeds and mix into marshmallow syrup.
3) Pour mixture into a buttered casserole dish or onto a wax paper. Flatten out the mix to 1 inch thick and let cool. Cut into 1inch squares.
4) Place two or three granola bar cubes into sandwich size plastic bags. Add a few pieces of each of the dried fruits to each bag.

You can make this without peanuts and use any variety of nuts, seeds, and dried fruit such as dried apples or dried pears. You can use raw, salted, unsalted, or roasted nuts. Don't use pepper-flavored nuts unless you like exotic tastes.

Recipe submitted by Robert Dukelow

STOLEN JEWELED COOKIES

Makes 5 dozen cookies

Preheat oven to 375°

Ingredients:

2¼ cups all-purpose flour
1 tsp baking soda
1 tsp salt
1 cup softened butter
¾ cup granulated sugar
¾ cup brown sugar
2 eggs
2 cups candied fruit

1) Mix flour, baking soda and salt in bowl.
2) Beat butter, sugar, and brown sugar in a larger bowl until smooth. Add eggs and beat well. Beat in flour mixture then add candied fruit.
3) Place by Tbsp onto baking sheets.
4) Place baking sheets in 375° oven for 9-10 minutes, until golden brown.
5) Let stand for 2 minutes.

Recipe submitted by Lauren Buckingham

Notes

Crisps, Crumbles & Nut Bread

Notes

BANG, BANG BLUEBERRY BUCKLE

Serves 8 to 10

Preheat oven to 375°

Ingredients:

1 cup sugar
2 eggs
4 cups flour
1 tsp salt
½ cup butter (1 stick)
1 cup milk
4 tsp baking powder
4 cups blueberries (or huckleberries, if you can find
   them)

Topping:
½ cup sugar
½ tsp cinnamon
⅓ cup flour
¼ cup butter (½ stick)

1) Beat sugar, butter and eggs. Stir in milk, flour,
   baking powder, and salt. Gently stir in berries.
2) Spoon into greased and floured 9″ x 13″ pan.
3) Combine topping ingredients using two forks or

a pastry blender. Sprinkle over top of batter.
4) Bake for 45 – 50 minutes at 375°.

In Idaho, where I once lived, we made buckles with huckleberries. However, they're not easy to find and you sometimes are vying with a bear for the fruit. I suggest blueberries!

Recipe submitted by Kathy McIntosh

BREAKING & ENTERING EASY
BANANA BREAD

Serves 6 to 8

Preheat oven to 350°

Ingredients:

½ cup shortening
1 cup sugar
2 cups flour
1 cup ripe bananas
½ tsp baking soda
½ tsp salt
1 egg
1 tsp vanilla
1 cup walnuts (if desired)

1) Mix together all dry ingredients in a separate bowl.
2) Mix together shortening, egg, vanilla and bananas.
3) Add dry ingredients to shortening, egg, vanilla and bananas.
4) Mix just enough so all ingredients combine. Do not over mix. Mixture should be thick.

5) Pour into greased and floured loaf pan.
6) Bake one hour at 350°. Test with knife or toothpick to make certain it is done.

Recipe submitted by Michele D. Peters

WILD BRONCO APPLE CRUMBLE

Serves 6

Preheat oven to 350°

Ingredients:

2 - 21 oz cans apple pie filling
1 pouch (1 lb 5 oz) Betty Crocker oatmeal cookie mix
½ cup butter melted
½ cup chopped pecans – optional

1) Spray bottom and sides of an 8" x 8" glass baking dish. Spread apple pie filling in the bottom of the dish.
2) In a bowl, combine the oatmeal cookie mix and melted butter until crumbly. Sprinkle cookie mix over the apple pie filling.
3) Bake at 350° for 30 minutes.
4) Remove from oven, sprinkle with nuts.
5) Bake an additional 10 minutes until the topping is golden brown.

Serve warm or at room temperature with ice cream.

This is the easiest almost homemade dessert I make and is so popular I can serve it at any gathering.

Wild Bronco is the name of the fictional restaurant in my books.

Recipe submitted by L. A. Keller

Pies & Pastries

Notes

BLUEBERRY TART TEMPTATION

Serves 6 to 8

Preheat oven to 400°

Ingredients:

1½ cups + 4 Tbsp flour, divided
¾ cup butter, softened
¼ tsp salt
1½ Tbsp white vinegar
5½ cups blueberries, divided (reserve 2 ½ cups most
  select)
⅔ cup + 3 Tbsp sugar, divided
⅛ tsp cinnamon

1) In a medium bowl, mix 1½ cups flour, ¼ tsp salt,
   3 Tbsp sugar and 1 ½ Tbsp white vinegar.
2) Cut in butter until mixture resembles small
   crumbs. Food processor works well for this.
3) Shape into dough and with lightly floured
   fingers, press into loose-bottom spring form pan
   (10") about ¼" thick on bottom and 1" high on
   sides.
4) Mix remaining 4 Tbsp flour with ⅔ cup sugar
   and cinnamon. Mix with 3 cups of berries.

5) Pour into crust and bake on lowest rack at 400° for 50-60 minutes or until crust is well browned and filling bubbles. Remove from oven to cooling rack.
6) Arrange remaining 2½ cups of select berries on top while still hot.

Cool before serving.

To serve, run knife around edge and remove rim of pan. Leave on bottom of pan and place on serving plate. Good served plain or with ice cream.

Easier to make than a pie and just as good. The fresh berries on top add texture and flavor.

Recipe submitted by Toni Niesen

DEATH BY CHOCOLATE TOFFEE TARTS

Serves 12

Ingredients:

2 pkgs - six Keebler Mini Graham Cracker Pie Crusts
2 - 5 oz pkgs chocolate Jell-O Cook & Serve Pudding *
1 level tsp dark, unsweetened cocoa
6 cups milk**
2 pkgs Heath English Toffee Bits
6 to 8 squares of semi-sweet chocolate bar
whipped cream

1) Whisk together cocoa and pudding mix in heavy saucepan.
2) Over medium heat, whisk in milk.
3) Bring pudding to a boil, stirring constantly. Remove from heat.
4) Cool 3-4 minutes, whisking twice to keep pudding smooth and silky.
5) Pour pudding into mini graham cracker crusts, just until full. Sprinkle English Toffee bits over warm pudding, evenly in a single layer. Chill pudding in refrigerator for 2 hours.
6) Shave chocolate bar into swirls. Top pudding with whipped cream and swirls. Serve cold.

VARIATIONS

Chocolate Mint Tart: Add ½ tsp mint or peppermint extract to chocolate pudding recipe. Follow cooking and chilling instructions. Omit toffee. Garnish with whipped cream, chocolate swirls and a fresh mint leaf.

Vanilla Toffee Tarts: Use vanilla *cook and serve* pudding mix. Eliminate cocoa and chocolate swirls. Sprinkle English Toffee bits on pudding before chilling. Top cold pudding with whipped cream and a few toffee bits.

Butterscotch Toffee Tarts: Use butterscotch *cook and serve* pudding mix. Eliminate cocoa and chocolate swirls. Sprinkle English Toffee bits on pudding before chilling. Top cold pudding with whipped cream and crushed walnuts.

Two-Tone Toffee Tart: Use 1 pkg vanilla *cook and serve* pudding mix and 1 pkg chocolate *cook and serve.* Add ½ tsp dark cocoa to chocolate pudding mix then add 3 cups of milk. Follow cooking instructions. Carefully ladle chocolate pudding into mini graham cracker crusts until half full. Place filled crusts in refrigerator to chill for one hour.
After chocolate pudding is chilled, cook vanilla pudding with 3 cups milk over medium heat. Bring to boil and remove from stove. Whisk pudding to assist in its cooling and keep smooth. Cool 5 minutes, whisking at least every 2 minutes to keep smooth. Carefully ladle vanilla pudding onto chilled chocolate pudding. Some vanilla pudding may flow into chocolate pudding. Toffee bits are optional. Chill for two hours. Shave chocolate

bar into swirls. Top with whipped cream and chocolate swirls.

*Do not use instant pudding mix, as the filling will not set.
**Skim or 1% milk results in thinner filling that doesn't set well.

Recipe submitted by Yvonne M. Corrigan-Carr

Notes

_____
_____
_____
_____
_____
_____
_____
_____
_____
_____
_____
_____
_____
_____
_____
_____
_____
_____
_____
_____
_____
_____
_____
_____
_____

GLAZED BULLETPROOF BLUEBERRY PIE

Serves 6

Preheat oven to 375°

Ingredients:

1 baked pastry shell (9 inch)
1 - 3 oz package cream cheese
4 cups fresh blueberries, divided
½ cup water
¾ cup sugar
2 Tbsp cornstarch
2 tsp lemon juice

1) Blind bake your favorite 9" piecrust and allow it to cool (see Note).
2) Soften the cream cheese and then spread it in the bottom of the cooked, cooled pie shell.
3) Spread 3 cups of fresh, clean blueberries onto the cream cheese.
4) Combine the remaining 1 cup of fresh blueberries and water; bring to a boil. Simmer for 2 minutes.
5) Combine sugar and cornstarch; stir into cooked blueberries. Cook until thick and not cloudy.

6) Cool the blueberry mixture slightly and add the lemon juice.
7) Pour the blueberry mixture over the berries in the piecrust.
8) Chill 1 hour before serving.

NOTE: Blind baking a piecrust.

1) Refrigerate the piecrust for at least 30 minutes before blind baking. This step solidifies the fat so that the crust doesn't shrink.
2) Line the crust with a parchment round or paper coffee filter or foil.
3) Add pie weights - dry rice or dry beans will work if you don't have pie weights.
4) Bake for 20 minutes at 375°. Remove the pie from the oven and lift out the paper and weights. Prick the bottom of the crust all over with a fork to prevent bubbles.
5) Return the crust to the oven and bake for an additional 15 to 20 minutes, until the crust is golden brown and delicious.

Recipe submitted by Sharon Lynn

SHOOTER'S SHOOFLY PIE

Serves 6 to 8

Preheat oven to 400°

Ingredients:

prepared single piecrust
2½ cups flour
1 cup sugar
¼ cup lard* (or Crisco)
1 tsp baking powder
1 cup molasses
1 cup hot water
1 tsp baking soda

1) Combine flour, sugar, lard and baking powder and set aside.
2) In another bowl combine molasses, hot water and soda.
3) Pour 1 cup liquid into a pie shell, then add 1 cup crumbs, then add liquid, then crumbs again.
4) Bake 30 minutes at 400°.

This was my grandmother's recipe; in those days, we cooked everything with lard. And yes, you can still buy it today in the store! (Though you'll probably want to substitute shortening.)

Recipe submitted by Suzanne Flaig.

THE PROOF'S IN THE CHOCOLATE PUDDING/PIE

Serves 8

Ingredients:

¼ cup powdered cocoa
2 cups sugar
2 cups milk
1 egg
¼ cup white flour
¼ tsp. salt
1 tsp vanilla

1) Mix dry ingredients thoroughly. Beat the egg well and mix with the milk then add to dry ingredients.
2) Cook over medium heat. Stir constantly*, until mixture thickens and boils with a dull "plop".
3) Remove from heat, add vanilla and mix well.
4) Pour into an 8" baked pie shell and refrigerate until set. Top with meringue or whipped cream.
5) Leave out the egg for chocolate pudding.

*Be sure to stir constantly. You don't want a scrambled egg in your pie. You may also temper the egg by slightly warming the milk before mixing in the egg.

This is an old family recipe that I reproduced in my fourth book, The Sky Took Him. The pie is simple to make, but potent. You must be an extreme chocolate lover to eat this. One of my brothers-in-law indicated that this pie is too rich for normal humans.

Recipe submitted by Donis Casey

TONY LaMONTAGNE'S SUSPICIOUSLY DELICIOUS PIE

Serves 6 to 8

Preheat oven to 425°

Ingredients:

1 cup brown sugar, compacted
1 cup water
1 Tbsp corn starch
1 cup ground or shaved suet**
pastry for a two-crust pie
whipped cream for topping*

1) Bring sugar and water to a boil and thicken with cornstarch mixed in 1 Tbsp water.
2) Pour into unbaked pie shell.
3) Sprinkle suet over the top.
4) Cover with top crust.
5) Bake until crust is pleasantly brown. Watch it closely while in the hot oven.

*Serve warm and top with a dollop of whipped cream. The dollop of whipped cream is important.

Purchase suet from your local butcher. It is the cow's purest and whitest fat (flavorless). On the farms, suet was always used in place of lard for richness and replacing moisture in game meat. It is an important ingredient in mincemeat pies. You may have to order it ahead from your butcher, although I've asked for it when entering the store and they have packaged it for me on the spot.

**I hold the suet steady with my fingers or a fork and shave it vertically, thin as possible, with a very sharp knife, removing any cartilage or gristle I find. Don't let the butcher grind it for you. His grinder may not be free of residue from the last grinding.

This is my Parisian great, great grandmother's secret recipe. It was handed down but never written down. Beware! It has no concern for cholesterol levels, but once tasted, nobody cares. It can be found in the early chapters of Vagabonds & Kings.

(Take heart! This will result in the most perfect pastry you will ever make.)

Recipe submitted by Merle McCann

Puddings
&
Chilled Desserts

Notes

BAILED OUT BAILEY'S IRISH CREAM TIRAMISU

Serves 8

Ingredients:

1 lb mascarpone cheese
2 tsp vanilla extract
⅓ cup sugar
2 medium egg yolks
1 cup heavy cream
4 oz Bailey's Irish Cream
1 lb Italian (imported) ladyfingers
3 cups cold, strong coffee
¾ cup shaved semisweet chocolate

1) Stir together mascarpone cheese, vanilla, egg yolks, cream, and Bailey's Irish Cream in a large bowl until well blend. Add sugar and beat until smooth.
2) Coat the bottom of a 9" x 9" pan with a thick layer of the cheese mixture.
3) *Quickly* dip the ladyfingers in the coffee and place in the pan to form one layer.
4) Spread a layer of the cheese blend, sprinkle with chocolate shavings. Repeat process until all the

ladyfingers are used, reserving some of the cheese mixture.

5) Top with remaining cheese mixture and sprinkle with chocolate shavings.
6) Chill 5 hours or overnight.

Imported Italian ladyfingers are firmer and drier than the variety in the US. US ladyfingers or small pieces of sponge cake or pound cake may be substituted.
If such a substitution is made, don't dip the fingers in coffee, but paint the coffee on with a pastry brush, to prevent them from falling apart.

As served in my novel, Revenge of the Gypsy Queen, a Tracy Eaton mystery.

Recipe submitted by Kris Neri

BREAD PUDDING WITH PROHIBITION WHISKEY SAUCE

Makes 20 good-sized pieces

Preheat oven to 350°

Ingredients:

butter or pan spray
24 oz bread, day old, preferably Challah or egg bread
2 qt light cream or ½ heavy cream/½ half & half
6 eggs
2½ cups sugar
2 cups raisins, plumped in brandy or hot water
2 Tbsp vanilla
blueberries and walnuts or pecans (optional)

1) Butter or spray 2" hotel pan (12" x 20" x 2" deep)
2) Slice bread into cubes and place cubes in hotel pan.
3) In a heavy-bottomed pot or pan, heat cream and sugar, stirring often until sugar dissolves; do not boil.
4) While cream and sugar are heating, whisk eggs in a large bowl until mixed.
5) Also have raisins soaking in liquid.
6) Temper the hot cream/sugar mixture by adding

a bit at a time to the eggs to warm it up. When it is warm, fully mix the eggs with the hot cream/sugar mixture (do this off heat).

7) Strain the raisins and sprinkle over the bread.
8) Pour the tempered egg/cream mixture over the bread and raisins. Let sit for 20-30 minutes.
9) Tumble mixture with fingers and then bake at 350° for 45 minutes.

Whisky sauce:
1 cup butter
2 cups sugar
2 eggs
½ cup bourbon, Irish cream, or rum

1) Melt butter in pan.
2) Stir in eggs and sugar. Continue simmering to thicken.
3) Add bourbon, Irish cream or rum.

Serve warmed.

Recipe submitted by Lisa Marie Martin

GUILTY PLEASURE FIGS AND CHEESE

Ingredients:

8 fresh dark figs (Brown Turkey or Black Mission)
8 oz. Camembert cheese (or other soft, mild flavored
cheese)

1) Wash figs. Remove any bad spots. Slice figs
horizontally into quarter inch slices.
2) Cut the Camembert cheese into 1-inch squares,
¼-inch thick.
3) Arrange figs on platter. Put cheese squares on
top of the figs.

Enjoy!

Recipe submitted by Robert Dukelow

Notes

ICED BY CHOCOLATE GELATO, DAIRY-FREE

Serves 16 (2 quarts)

Place ice cream maker into the freezer 24 hours prior to churning. Prepare the gelato 6 hours before churning.

Ingredients:

3 egg yolks
¼ cup organic agave or honey
⅓ cup sugar
½ tsp salt
2 - 13.5 oz cans full-fat coconut milk
½ tsp vanilla bean paste
½ cup cocoa powder, natural

1) Prepare an ice bath by filling a large bowl with ice and cold water. Set a smaller bowl inside the ice water and place a strainer on top of the smaller bowl. Set aside.
2) Separate three eggs. Discard the egg whites and place the yolks in a medium bowl. Whisk egg yolks and sugar together until the mixture lightens in color. Set aside.
3) In a heavy-bottomed medium saucepan, combine coconut milk, cocoa, agave, vanilla paste, and

salt. Bring the combination to a simmer over medium heat and cook, stirring frequently, until the cocoa dissolves.

4) Temper the eggs: once the coconut milk combination begins to simmer, ladle a small amount of hot milk into the yolk mixture while whisking constantly. Continue to whisk a ladle of simmering milk mixture into the eggs until about half of the milk is incorporated.

5) Reduce the heat under the milk mixture to medium-low. Whisk the hot egg yolks into the remaining milk mixture on the stove and return to a simmer. Continue to cook until the mixture reaches 180° or is thick enough to coat the back of a spoon.

6) Pour the custard through the strainer into the bowl set in the ice bath. The strainer will filter out any bits of scrambled egg that may have formed.

7) Let the custard cool to room temperature in the ice bath before transferring it to a storage container. Refrigerate until the custard is chilled, at least 6 hours, or overnight.

8) Once the custard is chilled, churn the mixture in an ice cream maker following the manufacturer's directions.

9) Transfer the churned ice cream to an airtight container, cover with parchment paper or plastic wrap, and freeze until solid, about 4 hours. Or eat it right away. Serve and enjoy.

The coconut milk adds a hint of flavor that brings out the chocolate.

Recipe submitted by Sharon Lynn

PLEA BARGAIN PLUM PUDDING

Serves 6

Ingredients:

1 cup clear suet, diced into small pieces
2 cups finely ground bread
1 cup raisins
3 Tbsp sugar
¼ tsp salt

1) Mix all. Chop the ingredients with the suet to mix it through.
2) Transfer ingredients into a heat-resistant bowl.
3) Stir in enough flour to make it stiff.
4) Place the bowl into a large pot containing 1 to 2 inches of water and cover. DO NOT use a double boiler.
5) Bring the water to a soft boil and steam 2 hours.
6) Check on the water level frequently as it boils and add additional water as needed to steam properly.
7) Serve with lemon sauce.

Lemon sauce:
1 – 3 oz pkg lemon pudding & pie filling mix (not instant)

½ cup sugar
3 cups water
2 egg yolks

1) Combine pudding mix, sugar and ¼ cup water in a saucepan.
2) Add egg yolks and blend.
3) Add remaining 2¾ cups water, cook and stir until mixture comes to a full boil.
4) Remove from heat. Serve warm.

I swear this recipe must have been brought over from England when my mother's ancestors arrived from Great Britain around the time of the American Revolution— seriously. Plum pudding was known as a long time British dish and I'm certain this wasn't one of those desserts swapped among tract-home neighbors in my childhood. Happily for my family, this ancient treat appeared during many Christmas holidays.

Recipe submitted by Katherine Atwell Herbert

SINISTER STRAWBERRY BAVARIAN

Serves 6 to 8

Ingredients:

4 cups fresh strawberries
6 Tbsp sugar
2 small boxes (6-8 oz total) strawberry Jello
1½ cups boiling water
5 large ice cubes
1 cup (6-8 oz) strawberry yogurt
2 cups whipping cream
1 small loaf angel food cake or ⅔ of a round one

1) Slice berries, reserving a few nice ones for garnish. Add sugar.
2) Dissolve gelatin in boiling water. Add ice cubes, stir and chill to consistency of egg white.
3) Break angel food cake into 1-inch pieces and set aside.
4) Whip cream until stiff peaks form. In a separate bowl, whip thickened gelatin until frothy.
5) In large bowl, fold yogurt and strawberries into gelatin.
6) Finally, fold in whipped cream followed by cake pieces.
7) Spoon into large clear glass serving bowl.

8) Refrigerate several hours and serve garnished with fresh strawberries.

Option: Spoon mixture into angel food cake pan and freeze. Unmold and serve frozen.

Good summer dessert to serve to a group.

Recipe submitted by Toni Niesen

TEMPTED BY TIRAMISU

Ingredients:

7 egg yolks
½ cup sugar
⅔ cup sweet Marsala wine
1 Tbsp Frangelico
8 oz mascarpone, softened to room temperature
1 pint heavy cream
1 cup brewed espresso coffee
1 ounce dark chocolate
¼ cup Captain Morgan's Spiced rum
1 tsp natural vanilla extract
48 ladyfingers (Italian name *Savoiardi*)
¼ cup shaved chocolate

1) Cream together egg yolks and sugar in a heatproof bowl set over a pot of simmering water.
2) Add ⅓ cup of the Marsala and continue to whisk until mixture is thick and doubled in volume. (This is basically a zabaglione). Remove from heat. Stir in the mascarpone until completely blended
3) In a chilled bowl, whip the heavy cream to soft peaks. Fold the whipped cream into the

mascarpone mixture, to lighten.

4) In a small saucepan, combine espresso, chocolate, rum, Fra Angelico, vanilla, and remaining ⅓ cup Marsala. Heat gently, and stir to dissolve the chocolate. Then, chill the mixture to cool it down, about 15 minutes.

5) Quickly dip each ladyfinger in the chilled coffee mixture and arrange in a single layer on a 9" by 13" glass baking pan. Do not soak the cookies or they will become too moist.

6) Spread ½ the mascarpone cream evenly with a spatula on top of the dipped ladyfingers. Repeat with a second layer of dipped ladyfingers and remaining mascarpone cream.

7) Sprinkle top with shaved dark chocolate.

8) Refrigerate for 2 hours before serving.

Recipe submitted by Howard (Doc) Carron

THE CLUE IS IN THE MOUSSE AU CHOCOLATE
(Classic French Recipe)

Serves 4

Ingredients:

3 fresh eggs at room temp, separated
6 oz bittersweet chocolate
1 tsp vanilla (or pinch of salt, or both, or a touch of caramel)
1 Tbsp sugar

1) Beat egg whites to stiff peaks while sprinkling in 1Tbsp sugar. Reserve the yolks.
2) Microwave chocolate until melted, no more.
3) Stir egg yolks into the *hot* chocolate. Don't worry if your chocolate seizes, add a bit of boiling water.
4) Fold the yolk/chocolate mixture into egg whites until blended. Pour into tiny cups.
5) Refrigerate 4 hours to set, then serve.

Store up to 4 days in the refrigerator.

Recipe submitted by Meg E. Dobson

Notes

Writing Tips Submitted by The Sisters in Crime Desert Sleuths Chapter Members and 2019 *WriteNow!* Conference Speakers

From Maegan Beaumont

1) Sit down and write! No excuses. Make it a priority. If you write just 1,000 words a day, you'll have a first draft in 90 days! 1,000 words is just 3-4 pages. That's doable!

2) Easily distracted by social media? Use apps like WRITE OR DIE and COLD TURKEY to keep yourself motivated and minimize distractions. Want to go low tech? Try a good ol' fashioned writing sprint. Buy an egg timer and notebook. Set the timer for an hour and keep track of your WPH (words per hour) that way.

From Meredith Blevins

Help. Where is the Beginning of My Story?

Where do you begin you story? With this: *'The trouble started on Tuesday.'* Begin your story on Tuesday, not on Sunday. Sunday is back story. (Be bold. Begin with dialog, if that feels right.)

When I'm honored to mentor a writer, we often see the first pages of a manuscript rambling around the block, shuffling their feet, and staring up into the sky. Waiting. Then we discover that the first sentence, and perhaps an opening paragraph, is on page fifteen. Eureka!

This wandering-while-writing must be quite old, because Homer pointed his finger at writers and said, "Begin the story *in media res*!" In the middle of things.

And remember—let yourself experience joy while you write.

From Lauren Buckingham

1) I find word sprints, such as the ones available on the NaNoWriMo website helpful. I find I get a lot more writing done when I set a timer and block everything else out, if even for a short period of time.

2) I keep "Idea journals", where I write down ideas, dialogues, or anything that could possibly become a story or part of one. And even when they don't, it's fun to look back on those!

From Susan Budavari

1) I keep a pad and pencil (and cell phone) on my night table to jot down (or dictate) ideas I have when I wake up. Often plots for new stories and solutions to writing problems occur to me during the night or first thing in the morning. Writing the ideas down when they are fresh in my mind eliminates the risk of forgetting them.

2) Keep a running list of character names in your stories. This way you won't overlook multiple names beginning with the same first letter and/or ones that rhyme or sound alike, or conflict in any way with each other.

From Bill Butler

As for a writing tip, I put the story down quickly. Then let it alone for a week or more while the details marinate in my head. Then edit, and re-edit until it flows and makes sense. If I'm lucky, an objective editor gives me feedback, which causes me to edit some more. Eventually, the story reaches the point in which no word can be removed. Then it is ready for submission.

From Howard (Doc) Carron

The most important factor in writing is research. Make sure you set aside the same time every day to write-even if it is only a paragraph. Finish a first draft before you start the editing process. Read the dialogue out loud when you write so that it sounds real.

From Donis Casey

1) Writing is like learning to cook. The best way to do it is to study the techniques of a master. When you first start trying to cook on your own, you may find yourself following the master's recipes, but the more you practice, the more you'll begin to deviate, to try different combinations and different methods of preparation and presentation. The day comes when your creations are entirely your own, entirely original, and the student becomes the master.

2) First drafts are usually a mess. Even Shakespeare's first drafts probably looked like the dog's dinner. But no matter how bad it looks, if you've managed to complete a first draft, congratulations! Writing is like any other art. It takes serious practice.

A man asked Michelangelo how he managed to get that beautiful statue of David out of a block of marble. He replied, "It's easy. I just chipped away everything that didn't look like David." It's the same with writing.

From Yvonne M. Corrigan-Carr

1) To write a fascinating scene, close your eyes and envision the entire scene. Run it through your mind like a movie. What do the characters do? What do they say,

see, hear, smell? Use all of your senses. Then, open your eyes and write the scene that just played in your mind.

2) End each chapter with a sentence that is so intriguing, or generates so much curiosity, the reader will immediately want to start the next chapter – no matter how late it is.

3) Write. Just write. Carve out a specific time and use it faithfully to write, even if you must get up at 4:00 a.m. every morning before anyone else in your household wakes up. Pick any time that works for you, turn off your cell phone, ignore everything else and write. Once you do it every day for 30 days it becomes a habit that you crave. And your story will get written.

4) The following books provide excellent guidance for writers.

On Writing: A Memoir of the Craft by Stephen King,

Writing from the Inside Out by Dennis Palumbo

Writing the Breakout Novel by Donald Maass

The Artist's Way: A Spiritual Path to Higher Creativity, by Julia Cameron.

Save the Cat by Blake Snyder

Save the Cat Writes a Novel! by Jessica Brody

Screenplay by Syd Field (Yes, it's valuable information for novelists, too.)

A Pocket Style Manual by Diana Hacker and Nancy Sommers

Then, add the books in your genre that win the major national awards each year to this list and read those. Study the way the authors craft their story, develop their characters, write dialogue, and weave the plot.

From Erynn Crowley

1) Don't overthink, just start writing.

2) Find a writing style that works for you and stick to it.

From Patricia Curren

1) Inspiration for characters can come from unlikely places. Be on the lookout for them. One of the murder victims in my next book is modeled from a man's fascinating obituary.

2) Some research questions can be answered through the Internet but you may have to dig deeper. Librarians are great resources. Also, experts on the topic you're writing about. Don't be afraid to ask. Most people love to share their passion.

From RP Dahlke

1) Between writing, I like to read the genre I don't write: Sci-Fi, Fantasy, romance and my favorite, Historical Fiction. I find that reading outside my genre stretches my imagination, gifting me with new ideas, novel ways to set up a scene, etc.

2) When I am writing and get stuck, hit a wall, come up blank, I go for a walk, look up at the sky and remember to breathe!

3) I have good editors for my books, but I always ask readers if they'd like to be one of my beta readers. Beta readers come in all sizes and abilities, from retired English teachers, to stay-at-home moms whose eagle eyes catch all those nasty little typos that can, and will, creep into your manuscript. I always credit these wonderful people in the front of my books.

From Meg E. Dobson

1) Every SCENE needs three reasons to EXIST or it doesn't deserve its position on the page.

2) CHARACTERS: Protagonists must protag. Make them layer by layer from outside in. Become them. Every character needs a SECRET and a FLAW.

3) AUTHORS are risk takers that find JOY IN WRITING. Keep your life balanced.

From Robert Dukelow

1) If you are not native fluent in a foreign language, and you want to include text in that foreign language in your book, find a person with native fluency to review that text before you publish that book.

2) If you are struggling to write, stop writing. Take a break, go for a walk, pull a few weeds, or visit an old person who likes to talk. Then when you feel like sitting at your keyboard again, ask yourself this question: Am I having fun? If the answer is anything besides a resounding yes, repeat step two.

3) Good writing comes when the characters you've created come alive. They fight with you, demand attention and prominence, call you names and screw up your carefully constructed plots. Scruffy subordinate characters come off the benches, usurp the role of your manicured major protagonist, take over your plot and dare you to keep up with their shenanigans as they propel what has now become their story to a completely unexpected ending. That's how to have fun as you write.

From Suzanne Flaig

1) Since I'm a pantser rather than a plotter, I've always liked this quote from E.L. Doctorow: "Writing is like driving at night in the fog. You can only see as far as your headlights, but you can make the whole trip that way."

2) Another favorite from Harlan Coben that also works for not-very-proficient cooks like me: "For those feeling discouraged: You're supposed to think you suck. Only bad writers think they're good. Press on."

From Connie Flynn

Punctuation controls story mood and can create magic with only the humble comma (the pause) and period (the stop).

Want a heart-pounding scary chase? Use short sentences, choppy stops, abrupt turnarounds, using multiple periods.

High energy and enthusiasm? Try using multiple modifying phrases, load them with commas.

Want a tender moment? Let sentences meander, omitting as many commas as possible and ending with a phrase that summarizes your primary intentions.

Then read each type of writing aloud and listen to your results.

From Dianne Freeman

When writing a mystery, plot the crime first. Even if you're a pantser, it will save you hours (days) of working through plot holes if you know the who, what, where, when, why, and how of the crime before you start writing the story.

From Denise Ganley

When receiving feedback, I always take into account what Neil Gaiman says, which I think is one of the best pieces of writing advice around. "Remember: when people tell you something's wrong or doesn't work for them, they are almost always right. When they tell you exactly what they think is wrong and how to fix it, they are almost always wrong." To me, this means I need to be open and listen to the idea that something is wrong in my story. But it also gave me the freedom to dismiss the feedback that didn't feel right, and to trust my own gut in solving the problem.

Be brave and be bold. You should be a little afraid of what truths you put on the page, but it is important to share them anyway. Your voice is valuable, and you have every right to put your story out into the world. And when you incorporate feedback from others in your process, and you should, make sure it clarifies your voice and doesn't replace it.

From L. A. Keller

1) Make the time to write. It's hard to allocate time in our busy lives. I have found that getting up an hour earlier five days a week gives me time to focus on writing without interruptions. I've written more than when I dedicated a full day.

2) Remember writing is a business. I struggled to convince my family and friends that my writing was not a hobby but in reality, a business. It's important to keep track of your expenses and to budget your funds as well as your time. No successful business happens without organization.

From Arthur Kerns

When you're writing and on a roll, then suddenly you pause because the perfect word escapes you. DON'T STOP! Type some XXX's in its place and move on. Don't break your rhythm. Later the word will come to you and you can go back and put it in.

From Elizabeth Remic Kral

Invest in a copy of *The Chicago Manual of Style*.

From Nicolette Lemmon

For Writer's Block – Jumpstart Your Creativity
When trying to push through to a deadline, even if it

is self-imposed, writer's block can set in. To get back on the horse during writer's block can be tough. So, here are ideas that can help:

1) Get out in nature. Take a short walk outside and make sure to relax to allow your senses to take over. You want to notice smells, look at birds, trees and people, as well as listen to the sounds that abound in nature. A favorite for me is to literally walk over and smell the roses at my neighbor's house!

2) Rearrange your desk. Spending a lot of time in one spot like writing at a desk reinforces mind-numbing habits. When you move things around, your brain is forced to engage to find things again and that helps activate your creative muscle.

3) Make a list of ideas. Even if you only have a few minutes, grab a notepad or open the memo app on your phone. Jot down 5 to 10 ideas tied to a theme that can be fun, even crazy. You can use a theme like "5 things I want to try eating this year," or "10 book titles that rhyme." The more of a stretch or outrageous the theme, the better to explode that writer's block.

From Deborah Lewis

The magic of chicken pot pie is that it not only tastes divine, but it also looks and smells incredible. When you craft your stories, close your eyes. See your setting, smell the flowers or alleys through which your protagonist walks, taste the gritty city raindrops on your tongue, feel the rivets in the hard-packed dirt underneath your villain's feet. Grab onto every sense you have to build the setting, to build the emotion, and to bring all the layers of your story into the readers' ears, eyes, and mouth.

199

From Jess Lourey (2019 WriteNow! Conference Speaker)

1) WORD COUNT VS. TIME COUNT WHEN WRITING

Always give yourself a daily word count. If you err and give yourself a time count, say two hours in the chair, you'll find yourself justifying "awful plastic surgery" and Awkward Family Photos as "legitimate research." It took me a year of flailing in this manner to update my method. Now, I write 2000 words a day, five days a week (with time off for good behavior), which results in two books a year.

2) WRITE YOUR NOVEL TO ONE PERSON

This second piece of advice comes from Elizabeth Gilbert, who was speaking at a retreat in the spring of 2015. A young author asked Ms. Gilbert how she knew which ideas to use when writing *Eat, Pray, Love* and which to leave out.

"That's easy," Ms. Gilbert said. "Every book I write, I write to one person. It doesn't have to be someone close to me, and they don't ever have to know."

The idea struck me as both simple and revolutionary: which one person am I writing this book for? Who most needs to read it? What parts of the story must they know? What won't matter to them? What tone must I strike? By selecting a one-person audience and writing to that person from the brainstorming stage to final edits, I instinctively know what to include in my novel and what to leave out.

3) USE ALL YOUR GOOD STUFF NOW

Carolyn Hart was speaking on a Malice Domestic panel in 2007. She was at the conference to accept the Lifetime Achievement Award, and over 200 fans packed the room. During the Q & A portion of the panel, one aspiring writer timidly raised her hand and asked Ms. Hart whether she should hold off on using all of her good ideas in her first novel because then what would she have left for her second one?

After some polite laughter in the room (which I didn't understand until later—the question seemed excellent), Ms. Hart said, "Use your good ideas now. Your brain will make more. I promise." Maya Angelou concurs in her famous quote: "You can't use up creativity. The more you use, the more you have."

Since then, I never hold back when I write.

From Sharon Lynn

Therefore, or *but*, instead of *and then*. This tip is about keeping the story moving forward. The current action in a story should lead to conflict in the following scene. As an example, "Johnny finds a dog, *but* his mother is allergic, *therefore* he starts dropping allergy pills into her morning coffee." In the example, every action causes something to happen that escalates the conflict. Rather than, "Johnny finds a dog, *and then* takes it home to his mother," which isn't as interesting. If a scene is followed by "and then" consider rewriting, removing or moving it.

From Lisa Marie Martin

Always proofread!

From Merle McCann

1) Let your finished work "rest" for at least a month then read and alter, enhance or cut as needed.

2) Do not use a comma before the word, "then." Example: (I prepared and served Mom's meatloaf then froze what was left over.)

From Kathy McIntosh

1) Make writing a whole body experience. Keep your chin up, your feet on the ground, your mind limber and open to new lessons and ideas, your heart set on the goal of becoming a published writer, and your butt in the chair.

2) Seek the line between stage direction and setting a scene. A character's movements should have a clear, discernible motive and be consistent with that character's personality. Especially with actions accompanying dialog, sprinkle lightly rather than season with a heavy hand.

From Catriona McPherson (2019 WriteNow! Conference Speaker)

I love my recipe contribution to this book—Six-hour Pork a la Hands-off Writer—for many reasons, not least because it's a perfect metaphor for my writing process. It takes a lot of time, but not *my* time. I write a first draft (no edits, no reading over), print it out then leave it alone for six to eight weeks. No peeking. When I go back to it it's no longer the thing I wrote. It's something I'm reading with a dispassionate eye. I can skim off the unwanted fat (it was necessary in the first instance, but it's not needed now) and adjust all the seasoning. I do worry when I hear beginning writers talk about editing as they go or even showing early chapters to other people. Lifting the lid and prodding while something should be cooking away undisturbed can cause all sorts of problems in what should be a straightforward dish.

From C.W. Miiller

When crafting a scene, take 10 minutes to physically sketch the location where character tension occurs. Press a No.2 pencil to a legal pad and transform the scene from dullsville to lavish, opulent. Immerse the reader, grounding them with rich detail and backstory. The idiom still holds true: a picture, even a rickety sketch, is worth a thousand words.

From Susan Cummins Miller

The best writing advice I ever received: You can't rewrite what isn't written, so finish that first draft!

From Kwinn Mitchell

1) Write in tight compartments. Focus on the scene in front of you and nothing else.

2) When world building, think of the world as another character. The world can create conflict as well.

From Timothy W. Moore

Tip on Research— Too much information can slow your story and lose your reader.

For instance, you learned procedures of a police department, an emergency room, or real estate, etc. and you're anxious to share this information with your readers. I found, to keep the story flowing you allow the procedures to fill in the gaps between your characters and your story.

From Margaret C. Morse

Read your story out loud and record it. When you listen to your recording, you will experience your writing in a new way. This is an especially good method to test the naturalness of your dialogue. Just the act of reading it out loud will give you a feel for smooth and clunky parts.

From Kris Neri

1) Before you begin writing your novel, write a dust jacket-type description of it. Effective dust jacket blurbs capture the drama, the fiercest conflicts, a bit of the storyline, an introduction to your protagonist and maybe other characters, and essential character failings that will trigger growth arcs. Not only does writing a blurb teach you what matters most about your own WIP and helps to shape it, there's an added benefit: you'll use great lines from it in your eventual query letter, and you'll have a start on a strong submission synopsis.

2) Good characters, like real people, rarely give themselves unconditional approval. For insight into the limits of your characters' self-esteem and self-approval, let them finish this sentence: "I'm good enough as long as I'm ____."

From Toni Niesen

1) Before ending your writing for the day, write the first sentence of the scene you'll tackle tomorrow. (Good advice gleaned from a conference speaker quoting a famous author.)

2) I can be a world-class procrastinator. This is the best method I've found to get around this problem.

I read somewhere that writers are most creative during the first 30 minutes they spend on a project. To keep from wasting this, I set a timer on the days I most want to procrastinate. I tell myself I only need to work those 30 minutes, but invariably once I get started, I don't stop.

From R K Olson

1) If you begin a sentence with 'Then,' reconsider. It's implied.

2) POV—Delete 'he knew,' 'he thought,' etc. We're already in his (or her, or their) head. And if we're not in his head, we can't know what he thought. Think about it.

From Dennis Palumbo (2019 WriteNow! Conference Speaker)

1) Writing begets writing. In other words, the more you write, the more you write.

2) Forget about only writing what you know; write what you *feel*. Emerson said, "To know that what's true for you in your private heart is true for everyone—*that* is genius."

3) Don't wait for inspiration, just start writing. In my view, action precedes motivation.

From Michele D. Peters

Be vigilant of the data dump. A data dump can slip into your writing without your realizing especially if your story requires a fair amount of research. Sprinkle the brilliant gems of your hard research very sparingly throughout the story in places that make sense and help the reader understand or "be in the moment". That certain detail may give your scene a sense of authenticity and help your created world ring true.

From Tonya Plank

I love this writing tip, from Walter Mosley:

"Forget about good taste and focus on what the world is really like."

"Many times I've been told by people I respect, 'There's too much emphasis on race in this book' or 'The government and the police aren't really like that.' I am asked not to stand down but to stand back—behind the line of good taste. 'Books are entertainments,' I am told

'No one wants to hear your ideas about how the world works or what's wrong with America.' Of course, they don't. The job of the writer is to take a close and uncomfortable look at the world they inhabit, the world we all inhabit, and the job of the novel is to make the corpse stink."

–Walter Mosley, "The Writing Life," Washington Post (2005). From https://crimereads.com/how-to-write-the-perfect-mystery/

From Judy Riddlesworth

Write your passion. Writing can be involved and drawn out. Passion and inspiration may carry you through.

From Debra S. Sanders

Keep characters authentic. Read your manuscript aloud while editing. If the dialogue sounds stilted, it will feel that way to readers, as well.

2) Weave the story so that it holds together and supports itself. Pixar's Andrew Stanton advises, "Don't give them 4, give them 2 + 2". A pattern develops and holds the story together.

From Steven Schwartz

1) Once you start a story or book, don't stop. Power through that first draft.

2) Write as if everyone you know and love is dead. Don't censor yourself.

From Margaret Ann Spence

1) We all know that unspeakable first draft must be cut, expanded, rearranged and otherwise wrestled into the best it can be. To aid in revision, I keep a "Leftover

bits" file. I copy and paste into it any thoughts, dialogue, and prose which might be used in revision.

2) If writing from several points of view, keep their scenes/chapters color-coded. Write a summary of the chapter's purpose on a similarly colored post-it note and stick onto a white board. Then you can review in a minute the rhythm of the book. This should not drive you crazy, however. Not all POV characters need to have equal time.

Notes

_____
_____
_____
_____
_____
_____
_____
_____
_____
_____
_____
_____
_____
_____
_____
_____
_____
_____
_____
_____
_____
_____
_____
_____
_____
_____
_____
_____
_____
_____

Index*

A
Apple
Six-Hour Pork a la Hands-Off Writer, 35
Wild Bronco Apple Crumble, 155
Woodchipper Chopped Apple Cake, 131

B
Bacon, 11, 57, 61, 65, 87, 89
Save Your Bacon-Woven Pizza, 33
Bailey's Irish Cream
Bailed Out Bailey's Irish Cream Tiramisu, 175
Banana, 145
Breaking & Entering Easy Banana Nut Bread, 153
Dinamita Deliciosos Frijoles Negros Con Fruta, 49
Bars *see also* **Cookies**
Grifter Grandma's Date Bars, 137
Beans
Black Beans
Dinamita Deliciosos Frijoles Negros Con Fruta, 49
Cannellini Beans
Ribollita Gone Rogue (Tuscan's Farmers' Stew) 79
Silence of the Stuffed Yams, 97
Garbanzo Beans
Frankie MacFarlane's Lime, Lentil and Garbanzo
Soup, 75
Green Beans
Any Night Alibi Crock Pot Stew, 71
Up North French Connection Potato Salad, 89
Beef
Alafair's Meatloaf, 17
Cop on the Corner's Favorite (Meatloaf), 19
Killer Italian Meatloaf, 21

* Note: For minor ingredients, only page numbers are listed.

Mackerel
Holy Mackerel, It's Grilled, 37
Mallow
Malicious Mallow Soup, 77
Marshmallows, 145
MEAT *see also* Beef, Lamb, Pork
Meatloaf
Alafair's Meatloaf, 17
Cop on the Corner's Favorite, 19
Killer Italian Meatloaf, 21
Shaw's Favorite Meatloaf Sandwich, 91
Molasses, 167
Mousse
The Clue is in the Mousse Au Chocolate, 189
Mozzarella cheese, 21, 33, 63
Mushrooms, 1, 19, 23, 81, 93
Chicken & Mushrooms Crêpes Conspiracy, 3

N
Nut
Breaking & Entering Easy Banana Nut Bread, 153
Nuts, 127, 145, 155

O
Oatmeal, 137, 155
Orange Juice, 10, 25, 29, 115, 123

P
Parmesan cheese, 3, 11, 33, 39, 57, 79
Pasta
Doc's Scandalous Spaghetti Fra Diavolo, 57
Mac the Ripper, 63
Murder on the Menu: Prosciutto Chicken, 11
Tortellini to Die For, 65

Y
Yams
    Silence of the Stuffed Yams, 97

Z
Za'atar, 37
Zabaglione, 187
Zucchini 47, 79

The Sisters In Crime Desert Sleuths Chapter would like to thank all of the Contributors:

WEIGHTS & MEASURES

3 tsp = 1 Tbsp
4 Tbsp = ¼ cup
5⅓ Tbsp = ⅓ cup
8 Tbsp = ½ cup
10⅔ Tbsp = ⅔ cup
12 Tbsp = ¾ cup
16 Tbsp = 1 cup

2 Tbsp = 1 fluid oz
1 cup = ½ pint
2 cups = 1 pint
4 cups = 1 quart
4 quarts = 1 gallon
8 quarts = 1 peck
4 pecks = 1 bushel

2 Tbsp butter = 1 ounce
½ cup butter = ¼ pound or 1 stick
2¼ cups granulated sugar = 1 pound
1 square of chocolate = 1 ounce

METRIC CONVERSIONS
(approximate)

1 tsp = 5 ml
1 Tbsp = 15 ml
1 fluid ounce = 30 ml
1.4 cup = 59 ml
1.2 cup = 118 ml
1 cup = 236 ml

1 pint = 473 ml
1 quart = 946.3 ml
1 gallon = 3.8 liters
1 ounce – 28.35 gr
1 pound = 454gr
2.2 pounds = 1 kg

OVEN TEMPS

Fahrenheit	Celsius	Temp
250°	130°	Very cool
300°	150°	Cool (slow)
350°	180°	Moderate
425°	220°	Hot
500°	250°	Very hot
550°	290°	Broil

ABBREVIATIONS

tsp = teaspoon(s)
Tbsp = tablespoon(s)
oz = ounce(s)
lb(s) = pound(s)
qt = quart
" = inch(es)
° = degrees

NOTE: Please consult the USDA "Basics for Handling Food Safely": https://tinyurl.com/jcx3lw4